When the War was over

Tales of a mid-century world

First edition 2012

ISBN – 13: 978-1466302068
ISBN - 10:1466302062

Also by Newcastle U3A:
The Snoring of a Thousand Men: **Tales of Wartime
Childhoods (Foreword by Fay Weldon)** 2009, 2011

*Cover photo: A tin of sweets, as given to schoolchildren to commemorate the
Queen's Coronation in 1953*

Published by Newcastle U3A (University of the Third Age)
1 Pink Lane, Newcastle upon Tyne NE1 5DW UK
Text in Garamond. Printed by createspace.com

In celebration of the Diamond Jubilee of

Queen Elizabeth 11

2012

Note from the editor

This is the second book of memories produced by members of Newcastle U3A. The first, *The Snoring of a Thousand Men*, recorded their anecdotes of childhood during the turbulent days of World War II. But the sixteen years following the war, the span of the present book, also have historical significance. The exhilaration of the end of the war in 1945 grew into early disillusion. It was reflected in the stinging replacement at the General Election of Prime Minister Churchill, the champion of victory, by the leader of a party that promised change and technological development. And these were indeed years of change. They saw the beginning of the Cold War, when Russia turned from ally to enemy, bringing fear of the spread of Communism from behind the 'Iron Curtain'. It prompted the international nuclear arms race (with the birth of the Campaign for Nuclear Disarmament), the competitive start of the exploration of space and the spread of applications of electronics, nurtured by the war, into our everyday lives.

The first decade after the war saw the creation of the European Economic Community, North Atlantic Treaty Organisation and World Health Organisation and the United Nations' Declaration of Human Rights. The British Empire's mandate was being morphed into a Commonwealth with the independence of India, Pakistan, Malaya, several African countries and the creation of the State of Israel.

There were dramatic social changes in Britain. Health care became free for everyone, the duty of local authorities to protect children and an X rating for films were enforced and Family Allowances for mothers began. The evils of racism were becoming recognised (although South Africa defensively imposed *apartheit* during this period), an influential report began the decriminalisation of homosexuality, married women gained the right to undertake professional, pensionable work and reliable barrier contraception, even before the 1960s 'Pill', gave them greater control over pregnancy. The Clean Air Act was passed, and the association of smoking with cancer became acknowledged.

The 1951 Festival of Britain boasted of the nation's talents and achievements and, gradually, ordinary households became owners of telephones, electric and gas cookers, fridges, washing machines and cars. Television began its take-over of family sitting rooms. Sporting records in running (4 minute mile, and 500 metres) and water speed were created and Mount Everest was conquered. The discovery of the nature of DNA initiated major applications in science, medicine and justice. Literary classics included *Animal Farm, Lolita, Good Food Guide, Thomas the Tank Engine*. Rock'n roll and jitterbug took over dance halls, new film stars blazed in colour, pop art and pop music broke tradition. With the accession of the Queen, the fabric of the new Elizabethan age was being woven.

Schools, however, were still in dingy buildings, children's prospects were defined at 11+ and much teaching was by drills rather than understanding. Childbirth outside marriage was shameful and concealed. Despite the 'pre-fabs' and new tower blocks, houses were in short supply after the bombing (although new immigration to England had just begun with the *Windrush*). We could travel abroad on the first 'package tours', but with very little money in our pockets. And wars (Korea, Suez, Vietnam, Iceland's Cod War) and Middle East unrest brewed abroad, as they do today.

We have tried to capture some of the essence of this span of years, and what they meant for young lives, by asking members of Newcastle U3A and their friends to tell in their own words their post-war stories. Although most are about being young in Britain, some tell of school-age adventures in Burma, Canada, France, Germany, India, Kenya, Malta and (briefly) Spain.

For older readers the tales will bring back memories. For younger readers it will be an entry into what many of the authors have called 'another world'.

Ruth Lesser

4

Contents

Foreword

Our earliest years provide the most vivid memories for many of us. I grew up in South Shields, next door to the Labour Exchange in Wawn Street. Long queues of recently demobbed servicemen waited to collect 'dole' and find a job. We had a downstairs flat: three small rooms with no hot water system, no indoor lavatory or bathroom, and a yard where a single outdoor 'netty' and wash-house were shared with the family upstairs. Every Tuesday morning, Mam boiled, possed, scrubbed, rinsed and mangled the clothes in this wash-house, and hung them across the back-lane or dried them in front of the fire if it was raining. This left little time for cooking so dinner – which was what everyone called our mid-day meal – was nearly always a large pan of pea soup and dumplings. The different food on the dinner table marked the day of the week as surely as a calendar.

Time was also framed by life in the street. The lamp-lighter came with his long pole to attend to the gas-lamps in the street each evening and morning. Horses and carts delivered fresh milk, sacks of coal, groceries from the Co-op, and Ringtons tea. On Saturdays the 'pop man' brought lemonade in his cart. Fish-wives from Cullercoats carried large wicker baskets of baked herring. Boys delivered morning and evening papers, and men came to collect rent, insurance, or contributions to saving clubs. A knife and scissor sharpener came occasionally and we loved to watch the sparks fly from his grinder. Pots and pans were repaired by a tinker who came in a pony and trap. Everything was 'make-do and mend'.

When the chimney sweep came I was given the huge responsibility of going into the street to see whether the brush had emerged from the chimney pot. Across the back lane was a Durham Light Infantry drill-hall. Sounds of the cadet corps being licked into shape reverberated from this most evenings. At weekends we lay awake listening to 1940s dance music from the hall.

The cobbled back lane was where we played football, cricket, lopakitty, kick-the-tin, block-the-bay and a host of other games at which I was useless. I fared better when we played at 'the bombed house' – a large Victorian mansion set in extensive grounds at the top of our street. The gardens had overgrown after the house was severely damaged in a bomb-blast. This was the place for war games: making bows and arrows, fashioning tomahawks from roof slates, digging trenches, making camps, or pelting each other with stones and clods of grass. I still have a small scar on my forehead. A little imagination or historical knowledge was as good as physical prowess in these games and leadership skills were acquired.

At weekends and in school holidays we roamed further afield for adventure: fishing for crabs and sprats from the seaweed-covered timbers of the Pilot Jetty on the Tyne; catching newts, frogs and sticklebacks in the pools at Trow Quarry; building rafts to sail on the ponds at Boldon Flats or Whitburn Colliery; trawling hedgerows around Cleadon for birds' eggs in spring or collecting blackberries and rose hips in autumn. My early interest in biology flourished and, oh joy, I was put in charge of the class Nature Table in my first year at Laygate Lane Junior School.

There was another education at home. My parents were devout Christians and Sunday School and Chapel played a big role in our lives. I listened to thousands of sermons and learned numerous passages of scripture in the incomparable language of the King James Version. I met my wife-to-be there at the age of fifteen but it took five more years before she became interested in me. Although I later lost faith, much that I learned and the love shown by so many people have been foundations for life.

Politics was equally important. The family were committed Labour Party supporters and I drank in fierce political debate across the kitchen table at meal times. The Durham Miners Gala was a high day every year. We travelled there by special train with colliery bands from Shields. Even as a child I was stirred by the passion of speeches from Labour Ministers and Union leaders.

One Sunday lunch – it must have been 11 July 1948 - my grandfather brought a large bottle of cider into our normally teetotal home for a special celebration: Bevan had launched the National Health Service the previous Monday. The mines had been nationalised on New Year's Day the previous year. It didn't matter that the only work that Dad could get at the time was as a meter reader for the Electricity Board at fifty shillings a week (£2.50 in today's money): the future was surely ours.

Late in 1953 the future arrived. It was my first term at South Shields Grammar-Technical School for Boys. The regular Biology teacher was off sick and Mr McCardle took the class. He ignored the syllabus and told us about a paper that had been published in the journal *Nature* earlier that year, explaining how scientists at Cambridge University had worked out the structure of a molecule called DNA which encodes our genetic inheritance. "This is really important: you're going to hear a lot about DNA" he told us. His enthusiasm is as fresh in my memory now as it was that autumn afternoon. I had the pleasure of telling him, almost twenty years later, that my first paper to appear in *Nature* had just been published.

In the present book these memoirs of life in 'Austerity Britain' are remarkable for several reasons. At home and school children experienced discipline and authority, but outside we had a freedom that most youngsters today can only dream of. Food was rationed, housing conditions for many were still grim, the nation was exhausted by years of war and hardship, yet as these accounts show, life was good in many ways. Even national service provided lessons for life.

Most young people were confident in the future and, although we did not know it, we were destined to become a privileged generation. The annual number of births peaked at just under a million in the late 1940s.

Millions of these 'baby-boomers' and earlier 'war babies' have retired, or are about to, and most have access to computers. These tales are the first trickle of what will surely become a flood of personal memoirs about life in the mid-century. They have the truth of living history. They provide an insight into how young lives were moulded by those challenging years of change.

There is much to learn, remember and enjoy here.

Professor Jim Edwardson
Institute of Ageing and Health
Newcastle University

To provide a context to the stories, the main national and international events of the mid-century years are recorded chronologically throughout the text. As far as possible the stories have been arranged to match this chronology, although many of them also include events over several years.

Anchoring the stories to wartime memories, we have begun with two very different reminiscences of the War itself, one from the West, one from the East. Many more such wartime tales can be found in "The Snoring of a Thousand Men: Tales of Wartime Childhoods", published by Newcastle U3A in 2011.

The War behind us

World War II

Main Allies: Britain and Commonwealth, United States of America, Russia

Enemy Axis: Germany, Italy, Japan

3rd September 1939	War declared, after Germany invaded Poland
10th May 1940	Germany invaded France
8th January 1940	Food rationing began in Britain
26th May to June 1940	Evacuation of British Expeditionary Force from Dunkirk
July to September 1940	Battle of Britain: RAF repelled German bombers
7th December 1941	Pearl Harbor bombed by Japanese: USA joined the Allies
14th December	Japan invaded Philippines, Burma, Hong Kong
Spring 1942	Mass exterminations began, Auschwitz
10 June 1942	Italy in N Africa, joined by Germany in December
24th December	Germans defeated at Stalingrad
16th May 1943	Allied victories in N Africa
July 1943	Allies invaded Italy: Russian, British and Indian troops entered Burma
6th June 1944	D-Day: Allies landed in Normandy
25th August	Allies liberated Paris
21st April	Allies reached Berlin
8th May 1945	VE Day (Victory in Europe)
6th and 9th August	US dropped atom bombs on Japan
11th August 1945	VJ Day (Victory over Japan)

Prisoners of the War

Stuart Scott

There is, of course. no age at which the experience of living through a world war can be considered an enjoyable experience but I think the period from four years to ten is probably the least worst. They were the years which shaped my life and the lives of my contemporaries: during our childhood we were, and continue to be, Prisoners of the War.

LEAVE THIS TO US SONNY — **YOU** OUGHT TO BE OUT OF LONDON

MINISTRY OF HEALTH EVACUATION SCHEME

Wartime evacuation could be traumatic for children. This poster from the London Underground was used by the Ministry of Health to persuade parents that it was necessary.

My father was in the Royal Navy in Portsmouth when the war began and because my mother was eight months pregnant and we had no family in the South of England I was evacuated to Basing, a village in Hampshire. I was dragged (literally bundled into a car by people I'd never met) from the security of family life in suburban Portsmouth to a farm worker's cottage in rural England. I don't think childhood trauma was taken very seriously in 1939, or perhaps everyone was just too busy with the war

After a few weeks I was placed in the guard's van of a train at Hartley Wintney Station to make my own way to Newcastle as my mother, for inexplicable reasons, had decided to take her new baby, my brother Douglas, to visit her sister in London. Someone must have seen me across London because I eventually ended up living with my grandparents in Byker and met cousins, aunts and uncles, none of whom I had met before. All of this newness was complicated by my misery and, of course, a marked Southern accent which was a continual subject of mockery, until it was replaced by a local accent.

However, school and the constant excitement of a world at war soon made me forget my problems – and it was exciting! I walked to school past a machine gun post at the top of Rodney Street which was unmanned for the entire war, but it was always there as a reminder of dangers ahead. Then through tank obstacles on Albion Row, and to school in St Michael's Road with a barrage balloon centre opposite. I was taught for a year in a two-storey tin building labelled Gas Decontamination Centre with a yellow square painted on the door which would change colour to warn of a gas attack. We were surrounded by war and rumours of war and everything served to reinforce our ideas that war was omnipresent.

Conscientious objectors to war sometimes gave important service in other ways. In Britain some joined the conscripted 'Bevin Boys' working in the coal mines; in the USA some joined the Civilian Public Service and became firefighters (see 1945 photo above).

Conscientious objectors were billeted in Ouseburn Road School and it was a rite of passage for Byker children to throw stones at them, shout "Conchie" and run away. There were Italian prisoners working very, very slowly in Jesmond Dene, and the Quayside was guarded by real soldiers with rifles and bayonets. One of them was my uncle who did this throughout the war but in later life would tell us that he'd taken his watch from a dead German officer. "Did you find him in

15

Northumberland Street?" was the usual family response.

There were air raid shelters in every back lane which were useless in the event of a bomb landing anywhere near but we didn't know that at the time. The air raids represented the zenith of excitement – out of bed in the middle of the night and running to shelter in the culvert which took the Ouseburn through Heaton and Byker. Looking back, that wasn't the best place to shelter as the main East Coast railway line, which the Luftwaffe spent years trying to destroy, was directly above it. And then the next morning scouring the streets looking for bits of shrapnel, bomb fragments or anything which would form part of your collection. I remember being pleased when, at the age of seven, I had to wear spectacles as this made me the ideal candidate to be Japanese in any game we played: it was well known that all Japanese were about five feet tall, wore spectacles and were cunning but evil fighters.

The terrible, cataclysmic events of the early years of the war - defeat in Norway, defeat in France, Dunkirk, the menace of U-boats, Pearl Harbor, Singapore, the loss of *HMS Prince of Wales* and the *Repulse* - seemed to pale beside our conviction that we were English and would therefore inevitably win, with a little help from the USSR and the USA (but they could have joined in a little earlier according to our parents).

When I think of it all now I'm reminded of a moment in Dad's Army when Captain Mainwaring decided to spend a few minutes explaining to his platoon the wider strategies of the war. "Hitler's across the Channel" he said, "still recovering from the bloody nose we gave him at Dunkirk". I think we all felt like that in class 3A at Raby Street Junior School, though perhaps not our teachers who must have understood, in ways that we never could, the realities of Britain's situation.

The war ended just as I began secondary school and the country faced the grim years of austerity in a society ravaged and destroyed

16

by bombing though less so, as we soon discovered, than Germany, Poland and parts of France.

My war began with the personal trauma of evacuation and it ended with my reaction, and the reactions of everyone else I think, to the newsreels which the government decided should be shown in cinemas for weeks, showing what had happened in Belsen and Auschwitz and Sobibor and all the other camps.

If I had to isolate the formative influences upon my childhood I'd say firstly my weeks of evacuation in Hampshire (where by the way I was treated with kindness – a very belated thank you to the Wilkinson family) and secondly the terrors produced by the films showing the camps. However, the liberation of Belsen and the others, together with the evidence at the Nuremberg Trials, did help to produce among my contemporaries the lasting idea that we'd been present at one of the very few "just wars" in recorded history. It's an idea which has been chipped away at by revisionist historians but it's still very generally accepted.

A Newcastle war memorial to the Royal Tank Regiment.

I entitled this piece 'Prisoners of the War' to imply that I and my contemporaries still carry with us the values and beliefs that we were given, or produced for ourselves, in wartime Britain. Clearly an individual's value system is made up of many strands so I'll conclude with only a few: a sense of patriotism (which can at times be unthinking), a feeling that the UK will somehow or other end up on the winning side and, allied to this, an acceptance that a recourse to State authorised violence is a legitimate solution to political problems. Would we, for example, have gone to war in Iraq, Afghanistan and Libya without the relic of our folk memories that, at one moment in our past, 'Might was Right'?

17

Escape from war in Burma

Peggy McCarthy

My parents went to Burma from India in the year 1923, taking with them a three months old baby, my elder sister. My two brothers, my other sister and I were born in Rangoon. We all lived in Rangoon very happily for many years until the sad day when the invasion of Burma by the Japanese in December 1941 obliged us to flee that beautiful country in early 1942 – a country which we had grown to love with deep affection.

Up to the end of August 1939, in spite of the disquieting accounts from Europe, we children gave little thought to the unrest that was gathering momentum on the Continent. Nor did most people older than ourselves, if it came to that. My father and mother went to a dance held by an Auxiliary Unit of the Royal Artillery, on the occasion of their annual prize-giving for shooting, which actually took place on the 2nd September 1939. It was at this function that the news was given by the Adjutant of the Unit that the Germans had invaded Poland, and that Warsaw was in flames. The celebrations were brought to an abrupt end.

On Sunday 3rd September everybody in Rangoon in possession of a radio was riveted to their seats. Those who hadn't a radio assembled outside newspaper offices. All were expecting a declaration of war. We heard Mr Chamberlain's announcement that Britain had declared war on Germany and, although this was expected, Rangoon and all Burma were electrified by the dramatic intelligence. And that is how we were ushered into perhaps one of the most momentous periods of our lives. Six days later my father, who was on the Reserve of officers, was ordered to report for duty. Being over the age for combat service, he was assigned to the Burma Censorship Department for the time being.

The New Year 1940 broke on a joyous note much as previous years had done. Except for accounts of the happenings in the faraway zones of war, Burma seemed to be little affected. Apart from the increase in the number of uniformed men who had come to strengthen our defences, we might have been living in the piping times of peace. Towards the end of 1941 it began to be borne in on us that Japan was going to extend in other directions the 'Chinese incident', as her long drawn out war with China was known. All the Japanese business houses, doctors, dentists and photographers were given orders by the Government to quit Burma. On the 8th December, Pearl Harbor took its place in world history. My father's commanding officer warned that dreadful events were likely to follow.

On the 17th December, the Japanese invaded Burma via Siam (now Thailand) through Tavoy. There followed intensive air-raid exercises, blackouts, hooded motor-car headlamps, and belated digging of slit trenches in every garden and compound in the city. Sandbagged walls and buildings began to shoot up all over the cities of Burma, in anticipation of what might follow. Rangoon and all Burma began to wear a wartime appearance – non too early.

On the 23rd December 1940, by which time people were again lulled into a false sense of security, we were all brought rudely face-to-face with reality and some of the horrors of war. The people of Rangoon were all bent on Christmas shopping, when at 10.10 the wailing of sirens warned of the approach of Japanese bombers. At 10.30 the bombs began to fall, and we were all caught napping in good earnest. The raid lasted nearly two hours, and an estimated 3000 people were killed in that period in Rangoon alone. We realised that our aerial defences were inadequate, and had it not been for the American Volunteer Group (AVG), who fortunately were in Rangoon at the time, many more would have perished. Fortunately my father and mother who were out in the city during the raid returned home safely. By evening Rangoon was counting its dead. It was a day of anguish, for many of our friends and acquaintances were among those who were killed.

On Christmas Eve we were informed by Tokyo Radio that the Japanese would visit us on Christmas Day at the luncheon hour. They were true to their word. We had no Christmas luncheon or dinner. The days and nights - especially moonlit nights – were nightmares. Raid after raid followed, and it was a period of running in and out of trenches at unexpected times. Bangkok, already in enemy territory, was only an hour and a half away and, although our warning system was quite good, we knew that our defences were deplorable. I forget how many raids we were in, but the number ran into dozens. On Christmas Day Hong Kong fell to the Japanese. Ominous news.

Singapore was taken in January 1942, and we knew that Rangoon was next on the list. Families were 'shifted' to Maymyo in the north of Burma. The Government said the "Japs will not be able to come that far". Our family, except my father, went to Maymyo. The Japanese advance continued. Mandalay was bombed as well as several other Burmese towns. At last orders were given for the evacuation of Rangoon. My father turned up unexpectedly one afternoon; he had caught the second last train to leave Rangoon. Within an hour of his arrival we had our first taste of trouble to come. A Japanese reconnaissance plane passed over Maymyo. The following day, Sunday it was, nine planes came over and bombed the hospital and some public buildings. Casualties were few, but we suffered the terror of the undefended.

Later in the week my father was informed that he could join a convoy of refugees who were leaving for India by one of the hastily constructed routes, and he was given official instructions to proceed into India with the family. Censorship was on the verge of collapse. On the 1st March, after inoculations for cholera, we entrained for a riverene port called Monywa, where we were to embark on an Irrawaddy Flotilla Company's launch for a place named Sittaung. The launch was overloaded, and it took us the best part of three days to reach this small town.

The evacuation authorities arranged for our onward 'despatch' through the Burma jungle and the prepared routes which led on to India and to safety from the Japanese advancing troops. Our progress was marked by daily walks of twelve miles from one camp to another. Twice we were held up for several days on account of outbreaks of cholera ahead. The end of each day's march was pleasant, as it meant a bath in the cool mountain streams that flowed through the country, and our daily meal of dhal and rice.

The evacuation authorities very accommodatingly confiscated our personal supplies of tinned food, on the pretext of distributing the pooled collection evenly en route. We never saw the colour of the labels on the tins, let alone the food inside. Our heavy baggage was carried by elephants up to the time we reached Tamu on the borders of India and Burma, from then forward by hillmen. Two marches further we reached Pallel, a tea planting centre, where we caught our first sight of Europeans after nearly 21 days in the Burma jungles. We were treated to cups of heavenly tea and biscuits by the tea planter, who then kindly sped us on our way.

Eventually we arrived in Imphal, a real Arabian Nights sort of city, with its minarets and temples. We spent a night at the rest camp, and thence by bus to Mampur Railway Junction, a hundred and sixty miles by bus from Imphal. In the meantime my mother had contracted the worst kind of malaria in the jungle, which showed up only after we had embarked on a ferry crossing the mighty Brahmaputra River, where we were to embark at a station on the opposite bank for Calcutta. My mother nearly died of this illness.

After an arduous journey, which somehow at the time did not seem so, we arrived in Calcutta, very tired, footsore, hungry and dirty. The trek to India had covered a distance of approximately

375 miles, which we did by river (Chindwin), over steep hills, jungle and rail. There was always danger of wild animals and herds of elephant.

It took nearly six months before my father was posted back to Military Intelligence. My elder sister and I did nurses' training; she joined the Women's Army Corps (WACs) in Delhi and served till the end of the war. My father returned to Burma with the Army on the reoccupation of that country and eventually was released from army service in 1947. It was at that time that India became independent and the family decided to make its new home in England.

A Stuart tank in the Allied army advancing on Rangoon during the reoccupation of Burma in 1945.

1945

	Jodrell Bank Observatory established in Cheshire
February	Churchill, Roosevelt and Stalin met at Yalta
	RAF bombed Dresden
March	**Last V1 and V2 rocket attacks in S England**
	British and allied troops liberated Burma
April	First Scottish National MP elected
	British troops liberated Bergen-Belsen concentration camp
May	Hitler and other Nazis committed suicide
	VE Day celebrated
	Germans left Channel Islands
	Reverend Awdry published his first children's book *The Three Railway Engines*
June	**Family Allowances Act passed**
	Demobilisation began
July	**General Election replaced Churchill as Prime Minister by Clement Attlee**
	BBC Light programme launched
August	Atomic bombs dropped on Hiroshima and Nagasaki, Japan
	VJ Day celebrated
	First Giles cartoons in *Sunday Express*
	George Orwell's *Animal Farm* published
October	France and (later) Japan allow women to vote
November	World Bank created
	Earthquake and tsunami in southern Japan
December	First post-war shipment of bananas reached Britain

Burma to Newcastle

Waveney Miller

Between World War I and World War II my father was a regular soldier with the King's Own Yorkshire Light Infantry. They had been stationed in Burma as peacekeepers and guardians of British interests against Burmese factions rebelling against their colonial status. Until the advance of the Japanese army through south east Asia, he had spent much of his time enjoying the pleasant climate and lifestyle in the garrison town of Maymyo in Central Burma, where my mother grew up. They met at the many social events at the garrison or hosted by her family, and were married at Rangoon Cathedral in 1940.

It was shortly after the birth of my brother, in early 1942, that my mother and her community were forced to flee from Burma. My father, staying behind, became part of the 'Forgotten Army', vainly attempting to stem the Japanese invasion. My mother and brother escaped to India where she was re-united with her mother and sister, and learned that her father and younger brother had been captured. My father was listed as 'missing', and it was at this time that, as an army wife, my mother and brother were evacuated by ship to England. They stayed with relatives in London who had left Burma before the escalation of hostilities. My father was found safe, and returned to England in 1945 to meet up with his wife and son before going on to Catterick Garrison in Yorkshire to await demobilisation and discharge from army life.

I made my appearance at the end of 1945, as my mother anxiously awaited news of family members and friends to find out if they had arrived in England or Australia, or been lost on the infamous trek out of Burma in 1942. Having been thrust into an alien environment, my mother, brother and I were then brought to Newcastle, my father's original home. Here we shared a small terraced house with the family of one of his sisters.

Probably my earliest and vaguest memory is of the 'pre-fab' our family moved into and of my grandmother, having reached England, arriving to stay with us and help my mother. Both had previously been used to servants. A third child was also now expected. My abiding memory of my grandmother was her frequent comings and goings between her four surviving children, unable to settle anywhere for long or to accept that her husband and youngest son had died in Burma.

My father found work in the shipyards in Wallsend, My poor mother, after my sister's birth, piled us all into a pram, and went to queue day after day at the local housing office in the hope of being offered premises large enough for the whole family.

Wartime prefabricated houses ('pre-fabs'), a few of which are still in use today in Birmingham, Halifax and elsewhere.

25

I'd never seen the likes

Betty Dawson

On an August day in 1945, it was announced that the war in Japan was over at last, and the world was at peace. A friend of my parents with her small daughter had arrived at my home in floods of tears. At last she would know if her husband who was fighting with the British forces in Asia was alive or dead. The Japanese had refused to give any information about their prisoners, and for four years she had waited. It took her another three months to find out that her husband was still alive – just. Four months later he was able to come home and see his little daughter for the first time.

Some of the VE Day crowds in London's Piccadilly Circus.

When my dad arrived home from work he told us we were all going to join in the celebrations that evening in Birmingham ten miles away. We all piled into our small car at about 6pm, but when we got a mile or so away from the city the only way forward was on foot. People were everywhere, laughing, crying, hugging, singing and kissing everyone. The streets were a blanket of bodies. With the little girl on my dad's shoulders and the three grown-ups holding tight onto each other and my brother and me, we joined in. I had never seen the likes of it in my 14 years – there were lights in every window and the church bells were ringing. During the war years it had been a complete blackout and church bells were only to be rung if there was an invasion. After some three hours we managed to make our way back to our car and home, tired but still so excited. I will never forget such a night.

After the war

Liz Lonsdale

'After the war', 'after the war' - that was the promise made to us that all of those things that we had asked for and longed for would be provided. What a disappointment! Nothing seemed different. Now aged nine I had moved on from a new doll: I wanted a new bicycle (or any bicycle for that matter), shiny shoes, exotic fruit and abundant chocolate. Now it was 'Later; you will just have to wait'. Yes, but for how long?

Most of my memories seem to revolve around food. I remember the enormous disappointment of tasting my first banana. I wasn't sure what I expected but not the strange half-sweet flavour with a funny texture. My parents weren't too pleased with my reaction. Bread was still rationed and we had to use BU's (bread units) for bread buns after school. Energen rolls could be bought without these but they had the texture of cotton wool.

The most memorable day was when sweet rationing ended. We queued for ages to buy a ¼ lb of our choice. What a problem! I based my choice on the length of time each sweet would last plus the sweetness. I shall never forget the taste of those Harrogate Toffees. Unfortunately demand outstripped supply and back came rationing.

Slowly, it seemed, fruit appeared in the shops but you still had to queue. Clothes rationing stopped and although the choice was limited we hadn't known better, so were happy not to have to make-do. I remember my mother buying a Dior style coat, waisted with a long swirly skirt - so different from those short, shapeless clothes. *Teenager* was a term not yet invented but we were aware of 'bobby soxers' in the USA. At fifteen or sixteen the only choice of clothes was the same as your parents. The

Hair on rods and rollers ready for perming.

standard was a smart suit, shoes with Cuban heels, twin-set and of course a perm.

I well remember the horror and indignity of going to the hairdresser, having your hair tightly wrapped round metal rods and the incredibly smelly liquid slapped on it. You had to sit with this torture for what seemed hours. Then, after the rods were removed, hair was rinsed, twisted into rollers and a huge helmet-like dryer was placed over your head blasting you with intense heat. After this torture your hair was combed and primped. A look in the mirror showed what a fuzzy mess it was. Of course you were told it would tone down in a few days but it never did. My friends and I would spend hours at home trying to emulate the hairstyles of our favourite film stars, without much success but it made for some entertaining evenings at no cost.

What did we do in our spare time? Cycling, walks and going to the pictures were our main forms of entertainment. First we went with girls then later with boys and eventually we were allowed to go to the local dance hall – grown-up at last. Most of our ideas and inspiration came from Hollywood; those brilliant blue skies, colourful clothes, enormous cars and dazzling smiles - how we longed to be like them. Gradually from the 50s to 60s, as more goods of every kind became available, life felt more optimistic as if good times were just around the corner.

Film star Audrey Hepburn's hairstyle was an early version of the Beehive that became popular in the 1960s.

A child's poem for VE Day

People in the street were shouting and cheering. I couldn't understand what I was hearing. I couldn't take in what the excitement was for, then someone said "It's the end of the war".

> I was confused, and ill at ease,
> I'd never known a world at peace.
> My life knew only nights without lights,
> neighbours together talking of fights,
> fights on beaches, in the air, on the ground
> in cities with names which had a very strange sound.

There was talk of 'the men coming home', husbands, brothers and fathers unknown, many a lass and lad talking of Dad they never knew they had.

> Watching everyone rushing, not understanding why
> and for the one time in my life seeing my mother cry,
> I ran away down the street and hid,
> for those tears scared me more than bombs ever did.

We played out in the street under lamps that were lit, no longer scared of our homes being hit. Adolf Hitler was dead, and we didn't care, as we skipped and hopscotched and ran everywhere.

> They laid tables the whole length of the street,
> full of sandwiches, cakes and jellies to eat.
> We all had a hat, and a flag we waved
> to show how joyful we were to be saved.
> Nothing to fear, no bogeymen creeping
> in planes and tanks while we were sleeping.

School went on without much delay, same old, same old, day after day, except for the things that appeared on the table, jars full of strange tastes, with stars and stripes on the label. So many good things but, I cannot deny it, I missed the Pom and dried egg of my wartime diet

> I got used to the buses being driven by men
> and young men being around our town once again,
> shops having fruit, and sweets not home-made,
> biscuits you put in a bag and got weighed.

There must be a hundred and one ways of remembering a childhood of post-war days.

Dorothy Connelly

From slates to fountain pens

Marjorie De'Ath

The year 1945 was a time of change. For me it meant moving back from my grandparents' house in the country to the small town, meeting for the first time my father, who had been away four years at war, and beginning real school. Today the small pupil visits the school in advance, meets the teacher, sees the classroom and is no doubt encouraged by a cheerful room with books and toys. I was expected to turn up on the first day, hang up my coat and my shoe-bag and begin work.

Few people had cars and there were no town buses, so you walked or cycled. At first my Mum took me the ¾ mile riding on a small seat in front of her on her bike. Other times we walked, and by the time I was six I was walking there and back four times a day on my own. When I was nine I cycled on the road, never on the pavement. Being met from school was a treat. I had no watch, and ran, skipped and walked along listening for the church clock chiming the ½ and ¼ hours and, oh, the panic if 9 o'clock chimed before I reached the school playground! I could take my time at the end of the day and varied my route through the churchyard or through the park. I had few fears of walking alone and only two small roads to cross. Once a man in a car offered me a lift, but I wisely refused thinking he might not stop when we reached the house.

We called the school 'The National', a title that looked back to its beginnings as a Church of England faith school in the 19th century. It was red brick, deep eaved with the second storey under the eaves and stood starkly in a tarmac playground divided from the road by tall iron railings and a heavy iron-railed gate. The boys' entrance and playground was to the left, the girls' to the right. The windows were set high, so only sky was seen by both teachers and pupils. Behind this was the 'Mixed Infants' where I began my schooldays. Inside was the porch where we hung our coats. To the right was the 'Babies Room' and the width of the building behind that was one large room which housed three classes each of about 30 children.

I spent only half a day in the Babies instead of the normal whole term. I sat at one of the small tables, near the coal fire and the rocking-horse and wrote my name and answered the easy sums

Writing at a school desk with inkwell: 1940.

written out for me (I had been to a 'Dame School' in the village). So after dinner I was led into the next classroom. There I sat at a two-person desk with a proper lid and inkwell and a bench seat that was attached to the desk and tipped up for us to stand. The desks were in rows facing the teacher; and so we began work. I was 4 years and 10 months old. We were taught as a class, sitting in our desks most of the time.

The teacher stood at the front and told us what to do, and wrote work on the blackboard for us to copy or answer. At first we wrote on a small slate set in a wooden frame, with chalk that made us and the desks very dusty. Then we advanced to paper and pencil, still using the slates for practice. The teacher would walk round to check progress.

We all followed the same reading book, reading aloud in turn as we were chosen. We followed a reading scheme just as infants do today, and learned from the blackboard the various sounds and combinations, chanting them all together. Then we wrote sentences based on the text. We learned to form letters the correct way and practised the curves and loops on the slate. This was *work*.

It was not designed to be interesting or fun. If you succeeded in your task that was OK; if you failed you did it again. I remember being kept in at playtime, puzzling over writing 'Old Lob' in my exercise book. He was a character in the reading scheme whose name seems to have been chosen to create confusion for the infant writer. There were no stars for good work, no charts to show how well you were doing just a tick and approval if it was right. We did not take our reading books home and, apart from them, there were no other books: neither picture books for pleasure nor information books to extend our knowledge or entertain us. We learned what the teacher told us, and no more. Sadly there was no cheerful atmosphere of children working or playing. Talking was frowned upon. We never chatted with the teachers but we were not shouted at or punished and I don't recall being reluctant to go to school. The atmosphere was kindly but strict.

There were other lessons, of course. We sang, and danced in the Juniors' hall. We did PT (physical training) with mats, benches, hoops, soft balls and bean bags, learning all the normal things children do today like handstands and somersaults. There was even a weekly radio programme, Ann Driver, for more imaginative music and movement. This was the highlight of my week. Every morning after prayers we chanted "This is my handkerchief. Blow! Blow! Blow!" and held up our (hopefully) clean hankies, and those without them were issued with two sheets of toilet paper to their great shame. Once a week there was News. You stood on a chair at the front of the class and told your news. I hated this.

Half past ten was milk and playtime. We were free to chatter and run and play outside. Milk came in ⅓ pint bottles with a straw to poke through the cardboard lid. It was delivered in crates and in summer stood in the relative cool of the porch to warm up, while in winter it was brought into the classroom and stood by the large coke stove that heated the big room. There the ice that pushed up the lid partially melted leaving it unpleasantly warm with ice lumps. I hated this too. The toilets were outside across the playground, quite open to the weather, except when you were in a cubicle, and of course freezing cold in winter. Going during lesson time was frowned on.

When I moved on to Junior school, we had our separate Boys' and Girls' entrances and playgrounds and did not mix out of lesson time. The first class was mixed: boys on the left, girls on the right, but after that we were segregated and in the last two years we girls had an overflow school to ourselves; thus we mixed with neither the boys nor the younger children.

Discipline was stricter and we were fearful of the head, Mr E, and some of the teachers. In Miss P's class bad behaviour like talking or failing to pay attention was punished by a ruler smartly across the palm of the hand. Once a boy who had committed a more serious crime, perhaps bullying, was caned on the bottom with some vigour in front of the whole school. Miss P also had a sharp

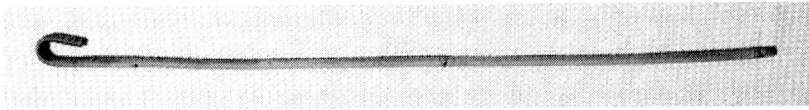

A bamboo cane.

tongue and few words of praise, and we were glad to move on to a more benign teacher There was, however, even at age seven, always that fear that something might be wrong and you would be punished as you knew other children were.

School hours were from 9 to 12 noon and from ¼ to 2 until 4. We said prayers on leaving at midday and again at 4 o'clock. The midday break was long as most children went home for a hot dinner. Mums were at home and Dads were home from work for an hour. There were no school dinners and if, as I did for a time, you took sandwiches you ate them unsupervised in the classroom. There were no after-school clubs or events like Sports Day or a Nativity Play, so we did not mix with other classes or see the teachers in a less formal atmosphere. We had no homework, and did not take any books or work home, so our parents had no involvement in what we were doing. Memorising spellings or poems or facts for a test all took place in class.

In class the only interaction was putting up a hand to answer a question, going forward to write on the board, or having your work marked. You did not say 'Miss, why does that number go down there?' or 'My Mum says you ought to........'. No one asked 'Why do you think this happens?' We did not discuss things either with the teacher or with each other. Silence between children was the norm and I recall being moved to another desk and partner for talking too much. We had lessons without any overlap of subject and were always taught as a class and worked alone. If you finished your work, you had to wait for the next stage. If your sums were right you read the big pre-war Rupert books from the cupboard until the class caught up or the lesson ended.

After the daily assembly there was Scripture. The vicar or curate came in weekly so in addition to daily Bible stories we learned about saints, the spread of Christianity and church history. I learned about the 'Synod of Whitby', without any idea where Whitby was. In the last two years we learned the ten commandments and the catechism. This was a church school and so you learned church affairs.

1950s knitting pattern for children's toys.

Every day there was Arithmetic and English and, to fill the days up, lessons such as History, Geography, Nature Study, PT and Dancing. We all enjoyed singing, particularly 'Singing together with William Appleby' on the radio. There was also a nature programme and a weekly service. The girls learned some needlework, and knitting. I knitted a dishcloth, the peak of my life's knitting experience. Art was also a

34

pleasure as the atmosphere was less laden with possible failure. We drew with charcoal and chalks on blue 'sugar paper', painted with paints mixed from powder and made patterns with little stencil sticks. None of it was *taught*. You just did what you could, and a subject was perhaps suggested. I do remember still-life arrangements made for us to draw.

There was no science of any sort. Basically we were expected to come out of Primary (Junior) School able to read and write and do all the arithmetic we were taught. It was thorough in practice but narrow in aim. It is strange to think that the only storybook we had to read was the class reader. Progress was slow as it was read aloud round the class and there were some very halting readers. A quicker reader simply read on ahead and kept a finger in the place: an enormous waste of time. The stories were traditional tales, fairy stories and classics re-written for children. I can't remember after the infant school having a story read to us. There was no reading book to take home and no library for us to choose books.

In our writing lessons we printed at first in pencil, but came the day, still in the first year, when we learned joined script with ink. This was not easy and the prospect filled us with fear. The ink was made from a powder and poured into the ceramic inkwells that rested in the holes at the top of the desk. It was sometimes badly mixed and lumpy, and also gathered dust and fluff over time to make it more difficult to get a clean writing line. One of the class tasks was washing out the inkwells at the washbasins in the porch. The pens were wooden holders topped with a metal nib, such as might be used today for calligraphy. Indeed this *was* calligraphy and the pen had to be held at a particular angle to form the letters. Sometimes the nib clogged up and made blots and sometimes the nib crossed and spoiled the writing. Blotting paper was a necessity. At first our

This modern version of calligraphy by Denis Brown is rather more advanced than would have been expected at Marjorie's school.

hands were always very inky. The upstroke, like the left part of the *A*, was thin, and the down stroke of, for instance, the *t* was thick and straight. *W* was thick down, thin up, thick down, thin up. The writing was curvy and loopy and within each word the pen was not lifted from the page and letters were joined with a thin up stroke.

A halfpenny in pre-decimal coinage was about the same size as a modern two-penny coin. The coin above dates from 1860 and was still valid until 1969. It was worth 1/480th of a £, and (unsurprisingly) had fallen out of common use by then.

Fountain pens were allowed later and so easy, but biros had not yet been invented.

We were taught Arithmetic rather than Maths. Teaching concentrated on remembering fact and method rather than understanding. Although, for instance, we learned to manipulate fractions they were to me symbols rather than a description of real things like half a cake or three quarters of

Sum-it: a card game to practise money sums (but not at school!).

36

£1 and 10/- were paper notes not coins that were valid till 1969 (10/-) and 1988 (£1). The note above is a forgery made by Germany during the War with the aim of destabilising British currency.

How to do your money sums

First chant and learn your Pence Table: "24 pence is 2 shillings, 30 pence is 2/6d, 36 pence is 3 shillings" and on and up to "80 pence is 6/8d, 100 pence is 8/4d, 120 pence is 10 shillings" (this gets you half way to a £).

Then change your pounds into shillings and shillings into pence. Thus, with 20s (shillings) in a £1, and 12d (pence) in a shilling, you were constantly changing your *s* to *d* or to £ during the calculation. For example, £5/11/4 divided by 4, meant first of all carrying over £1 converted into 20/-, and adding it to the 11/- to make 31/-. Then carrying over 3/- converted into 36d and adding that to the 4d to make 40d. The answer is £1/7/10.

a group of people. I was much older before I saw that ¼ x ½ meant 'What is a quarter of a half?' We didn't see diagrams to show what this meant. Although we chanted our tables, and like most people of my age I remember them today, I didn't see six groups of eight things in 6 x 8, just numbers to be learned.

In our pre-decimal age we had to deal with non-decimal money, weights and measures and they all had to be added, subtracted, multiplied and divided (see box). Weights had the same problem as money, with 16oz (ounces) to 1lb (pound), 14lbs to 1 stone, 8 stones to 1cwt (hundredweight) or 112 lbs to 1cwt, 20 cwt to one ton. We did not plan to become coal merchants or hauliers, but had to learn it all the same. We still have our miles today, but children learn the rest of measurement in metres and

37

centimetres. We had 12 inches to 1 foot, 3 feet to 1 yard, 1760 yards to a mile. So to add 3ft 6ins to 4ft 9 ins giving the answer in yards meant changing 15 inches to feet to carry over 1foot and so on, giving an answer of 1yd 2ft 3ins. No wonder we had little time for other subjects.

The playground was where we came to life. The boys in their separate area played football or cricket, marbles, chasing games, cowboys and Indians and Batman and Dick Barton. Of course there was endless re-living of aerial dog-fights with eeeeeeer! noises and the ahahahahahah! noise of machine guns. There was no television to base games on, but many of us went to Saturday morning cinema and they copied the films.

We girls played many different games with small balls such as Donkey where the ball is bounced up a wall and you jump over it so the one behind catches it. There were chasing games: Tiggy, Chain Tiggy, Relievo. Hide and Seek games like Block where the girl who is *It* defends her base against the rest of the group. There were many skipping games: plain jumping over the rope held by two girls, 'Over the Moon and Under the Stars', and 'Snakes' where the rope was swished back and forth. We knew many skipping rhymes, passed down from older to younger girls: *'Teddy bear, teddy bear, touch the ground','I am a girl guide dressed in blue; these are the actions I can do'*. Large groups joined in singing circle games like *'Poor Mary sat a weeping' 'The wind, the wind, the wind blows high', 'Pulcinella little fellow'* and *'The farmer's in his den'*. We also had our own made-up games involving chasing and capturing. We spent much time running about and very little in being ladylike. I was always eager to get back to school so as not to miss anything.

During the two years I stayed at school for lunch with my sandwiches we were quite unsupervised. We would go across the road to the church and explore the churchyard. We played hide and seek among the graves, or climbed on them and jumped from one to another. Or we walked down to the main road and bought sweets from the shop.

38

School in those very early post-war days was like everything post-war: still with its feet in the pre-war world, poorly equipped, unable yet to move on. I think we were more docile, obedient children, more accepting of rules and boredom. And even at 11 we were very much *children*, with no wish to be grown-up, and little interest in grown-up things. The knowledge we gained was pitiful compared to what children know today, even discounting technology like computers and calculators.

Marjorie in her school uniform.

But we were given a good grounding in basics like grammar and arithmetic and most of us could read. And we were happy with our lot if we got our sums right, if we got 10 out of 10 for some work, if we had friends to play with at playtime and if we had families and friends to go home to.

Heating, eating, learning

Alec Bamford

In Northamptonshire we lived next to the Methodist Church with its adjoining schoolroom which ran at right angles to the main church. Heating was provided from hot water running through a pair of parallel pipes, about 9 inches (20 cm) diameter, which ran above the skirting board all round the walls. There was a large boiler in an outhouse heated by a coke fire which had to be lit between six and seven am, usually by the same person. There was much relief when an electrically heated boiler was put in, only needing the settings checked and a switch to operate. The back of the school room ran beyond the side of the church and at the join the pipes were led through to the church which had a floor higher than the school-room so there was a cosy seat at the side of the room where this happened. The top of the bend was at about elbow height for an adult. By the time of the evening service and with a good congregation it was quite warm, especially for the long Carol Service.

I was attending the village school, held in this room adjoining the church, when school dinners were first introduced. As the school had neither dining room nor kitchens the hot food was brought out to us from a central preparation point. At first it arrived in covered aluminium containers in an ex-army vehicle, the kind with a framework with canvas covering, a bit bigger than a jeep. The teachers dished up at the queuing line, with the male teacher in charge of the meat. After dinner, the driver collected the dishes and allowed as many as possible of us to clamber in the back to ride up the hill to where the village road met an A road. We sang all the way, particularly *She'll be coming round the mountain* and its various verses, all with the refrain. All too soon we had a new driver with a 'proper' van, all shut in and the back door locked and our rides were over.

The village school had a set of cycle racks with space for at least twenty bicycles, but I only recall two of the 'big boys' ever bringing a bike to school. The rest of us walked, even the children from farms a mile or a bit more away. The school also served as a branch of the County Library. A box of books for adults and children was delivered once a month. The same master who dished up the meat was librarian, opening for an hour or so after school – I suppose it was more than once a month – and so I was introduced early to library tickets and library loans.

The nearest secondary schools were in a small town four miles away and a larger town eight miles away, one of which was the Grammar School. Most of the village children stayed at the village school till the leaving age of 14. The Grammar School was still fee-paying as I neared 11, the entry age. A handful of pupils were entered for 'The Scholarship' (the entrance examination for Grammar Schools). It was the custom of the village headmaster to enter one or two promising pupils a year early so that they would be used to the idea and 'pass' - ie be accepted for a free place - the next year, so maintaining his reputation. This backfired from time to time with only the fee-paying triallists passing and special coaching had to be given to one or two pupils for the next year. At age about 11, only a few of us continued at the Grammar school eight miles away.

Going to Grammar School involved being at the single bus stop for the morning bus time-tabled for 8.10 am, but known to race by as the church clock struck eight. The next direct bus was at 6.10 in the afternoon. School ended at 4, the bus home left at 4.25, the next (after the office workers had finished) well after 6.00. There was a long wait if you missed the bus and the fish-and-chip shop was out of bounds.

The 'Country Boys' had school dinners in a dining room with its own kitchen, but with the influx from London at the time of the V1 and V2 rockets a classroom of us had to take sandwiches in turn.

If we wanted to go into town, we had to queue to get permission from the Master-on-Duty, giving the reason. Some let us through on the nod, but there was one who conducted a thorough questioning. There were many US soldiers stationed nearby and one had a supply of empty flour-sacks which he sold off on Friday market days. These sacks were made into tea-towels and pillow-cases. The detailed questioning master was on duty the Friday I had to go to the market to buy a load of these sacks for my aunts and my mother. After listening to the details, he said he would have to tell his wife. This questioning was the only time I remember him softening his usual attitude. When my mother died aged 96 in 2003, she still had in use some of her flour-sack pillow-cases and tea-towels - one of the latter was quite ragged with about half the material worn or washed away. I kept that piece of tea-towel as a family memento: there was, of course, a drawer full of new tea towels with designs or pictures on them.

The only WH Smith's shop was on the station platform. This gave us a reason for being at the station to pass the time watching the trains, otherwise we played or stood about in the yard. When the bell rang we lined up in the yard under the care of our form prefect and only moved off into the buildings when given permission by Staff. On wet days we crowded into the cloakroom. Across the yard from the main blocks were 'the huts', three temporary classrooms built at the end of WW1. They were heated by coke-fired tortoise stoves. The tops were very hot and excellent for testing (in the brief time we were unattended between lessons and before afternoon school) the effect of heat on various materials, particularly the 'Celluloid' of set-squares and protractors.

A tortoise stove, so called because of the shape of the lid.

Rearranging my bookshelves about the time we were thinking of producing this book, I found a slide-rule and it made me think of the way 'doing sums' had altered. First there was mental arithmetic (all in the head), followed by mechanical (written on paper). At Grammar School I met four-figure logarithms, then I had a book of five-figure ones and later a hardback book of seven-figure ones. At the time of the four-figure logs I had my first slide rule (see right). In the 1950s as a lab boy in an Analytical Lab I used a mechanical calculator. Numbers were set by lining up levers in the correct place. Turning the handle once away from you did additions and turning towards you was subtraction. For multiplication the handle was turned away from you the number of times required. Fortunately there was a shift key for the tens

Slide-rules had three main parts: the main body with scales A and D, the central slide with scales B and C and a transparent runner. To multiply 2 x 8, you'd move the slide so that the C scale was in line with 2 on the D scale, then read the answer on the D scale. Division was the reverse. It was also used for decimals, square roots, cubes, etc. (Caption by courtesy of Geoffrey Drew)

and hundreds etc so to multiply by 532 for example needed ten turns only. Next I used an electrically-operated calculator which was noisy and shook the bench as it rattled away. Then came pocket electronic calculators. After that I had a programmable pocket electronic calculator which was great fun to use: tell it what to do with a complicated mathematical equation, enter the start data, push a key and there was the answer - no logs, no slide-rule, no bit-by-bit work keeping a list of the intermediate answers. In hardly any time after that computers and spreadsheets became available.

Scholarship girl

Sylvia Guilleminot

Out of a year-group of over a hundred eleven-year-olds, when the war ended in 1945, only twelve of us passed the scholarship examination for entry to the local Grammar School. In Chester-le-Street, County Durham, our little lives had been relatively untroubled: no bombs, no evacuations, few hardships. We had in fact experienced few strictures, little more than the wartime economies. We were living with rationing, a shortage of most commodities, shelters in the garden (huge ones in the school yard), identity disks and gas masks (unused); but we didn't starve, although school dinners didn't exist, and we certainly enjoyed life. The end of the war was a joyous time with street parties at home. At school we eleven-year-olds distributed a package to each child, containing Horlicks tablets and barley sugars. They had obviously been stored away in case of long periods in the shelters, but we had only sat in these once for practice. Now we were leaving for a new school with great anticipation and excitement. A Grammar School with its uniforms, satchels, fountain pens and sports gear was awaiting us. I personally had huge regrets because my best friend, June, had not 'passed' and would go to the Secondary Modern School. My mother was so proud. We were a working-class family, and I was the first to pass the scholarship. She worked hard to ensure that I should have everything required. Much of the uniform came from a very old-fashioned haberdashery, but the precious cream blouses were purchased in Jenners in Edinburgh when we were on holiday there – such delight. Of course the first day was bewildering. We

VE Day street party on South Street: Sylvia is at the far end of the table: her mother is just getting into the photo at the far right.

followed a long tree-lined drive to a beautiful building with playing fields. Then came the whole paraphernalia of locker-rooms, hooks, huge toilets, teachers in gowns, a vast hall, and the sudden realisation that there were pupils there who were just about adult. We had been in the top class and now were the lowest of the low. Then came division into classes. To my chagrin I was placed in 1B. There were boys and girls from local villages, mainly from mining families; there were professionals' children and ordinary ones like myself. There were prefects, timetables and individual teachers for each subject. There were school dinners and scholars' busses to take us home. What an enormous change! After about a month, however, we made new friends, acclimatised to the system and took it all in our stride.

The aftermath of the war still affected us. Food shortages meant that our school dinners were appalling, both in quantity and quality, whether you paid 4d or 5d a day (about 2p in today's decimal money). PE (Physical Education) lessons required us to wear appropriate tunics, all to be created from blackout material ornamented with coloured braid. But now, in the large number of exercise books we received, we did not have to write in the margins, as in primary school. It was exciting learning to speak French, to play hockey, netball and rounders, to read set books and discuss them, to sing in a school choir and to admire and idolise older boys and girls.

It was a good school with a strong academic record, firm but fair discipline and traditional activities. There I spent eight years growing in confidence and learning. I am grateful for my time in both primary and grammar school, and consider myself fortunate to have experienced them. I shared in the wonderful atmosphere of hope and anticipation in that post-war era. Peace had been restored to the world; one had freedom to achieve whatever one wanted.

This huge move was my beginning.

Shortages in Germany

Christa Clemmetsen

School for me started in 1945, just as the war came to a close. I grew up in Hamburg and at that time the shortage of teachers meant that we had a shift system: half the children went in the morning, the other half in the afternoon. As this was still a time of shortages, I remember having to go out into the countryside to collect acorns (to feed pigs), blackberry leaves (no idea for what purpose), and beech kernels (again for animal feed). All these were handed in at school.

I was taken to school on the first day and, when we emerged at midday, mothers were waiting to hand over the *cone*. This is a German custom, where children are given a large colourful paper cone, filled with goodies – not too exciting in those days, compared what they would contain nowadays. From the second day onwards we walked by ourselves. This meant a 20 minute walk for me but, of course, there was very little traffic in those days.

We were quite in awe of our teachers. At the beginning of class, everyone would rise and say 'Good morning'. I cannot remember that discipline ever was a problem. Naturally I would have been left-handed, but that was not permitted in those days and we were made to change to writing with the right hand. I believe that explains my untidy handwriting in some way, but it did have advantages, as I could write with my left when my right hand was injured.

In large towns like Hamburg there was a great food shortage. My family lived on the outskirts and we had a large garden, hence always had something to eat. However, we still helped relatives from the town when it came to harvest time. After farmers had harvested potatoes, word went round that on a given day at a certain time a field would be 'open'. Many people came by train and waited patiently for the farmers to depart. We then formed a line and began digging over the field again with small forks to find any potatoes left behind. Just as in Britain, we had coupons and whenever a shop had a delivery of something, mothers and children went off to queue in the hope of getting at least a little.

There were special recipes, describing how to make all sorts of nourishing dishes out of very little or items that would normally not have been used. I remember when maize bread became available. It was made largely from sweet corn and had a slightly yellow colour. At the beginning everyone was over the moon but before long, we got fed up with this. Unlike normal bread it seems to have too much of its own taste.

A German Kochkiste or hay box: food was boiled and put in the box to cook by residual heat for several hours – a big saving of fuel.

Many dishes needed a long time cooking or it was more convenient if the family was working in fields or gardens. So we used a hay box. The food (mostly some type of stew) would be boiled up and then transferred to the hay box to continue simmering for hours.

As a child I cannot remember ever going into a shop for items of clothing. My mother made everything. Occasionally she had help from a *Hausschneiderin* (home dressmaker). This seems to have been something quite common. In order to earn a little money, these ladies would come for the day and do whatever was needed: turn sheets, make 'new' clothes out of old ones, mend, patch and generally transform our wardrobe. After the end of the war red German flags (swastika removed) were handed out and nearly all the little girls had at least one bright red item. I remember that my mother learned how to smock, to give it a little character. I was confirmed in 1953 and for this occasion the *Hausschneiderin* made me a navy blue dress with a detachable white collar. This became my 'best' dress for all occasions like birthday parties or visits to the theatre. When I was 17 my mother parted with a grey velvet dress which, between the two of us, we made to fit me. After three years of the navy item, I felt very grown up all of a sudden. Contrasting this with the overwhelming choice children have today often makes me wonder whether we were less happy. Of course I would have loved to be able to choose something in a shop, perhaps something bright and a little different, but, as we were all in the same position, it never became an issue. Designer labels, *Bob the Builder* and *Hello Kitty* had not even been thought of in those days.

Today children and adults are surrounded by gadgets. Most people carry a little black box around with them, or hold it to their ears so that they can be connected at all times. Technically speaking we were not connected at all. When I was little we had a radio in the house and by the late forties my mother got a rather primitive washing machine – the wringer was still hand-operated, mostly by me.

A portable wind-up record player for vinyl 78 rpm records. Long playing records (45 rpm) were introduced in 1945.

In 1953 (my 15th birthday reminds me of the date) my parents bought a record player which allowed us to play the four records my mother still had from pre-war times. The highlight of my birthday party was waltzing around to the sound of the Blue Danube.

The next technical item to invade the house was a telephone. After a friend and I had spent some considerable time doing our maths homework together on the phone, we both were banned from using it for anything but the briefest of conversations. I think TV must have arrived in the mid-fifties as I remember a radio shop halfway to the village (a thirty-minute walk away). We would run all the way to the Youth Club meetings in order to save a little time, which we would spend glued to this shop window and watching the tiny TV.

In 1956 I came to Bournemouth to attend an English course. I lived with a family who actually had their own TV. Their friends next door did not yet have a set and the nightly routine was for the neighbours to come round after dinner. Everyone would sit in a row opposite the set with just a small table lamp in the corner. Not a word was spoken and at 9pm tea would be handed round, passed from hand to hand without ever taking one's eyes off the film.

After a few weeks of this I started going out at night with my new friends but my landlady could not understand this at all: "But you are going to miss ....!" Sunday dinner always coincided with Billy Cotton's call "Wakey, wake-aaay!" followed by his signature tune *Somebody stole my gal.* In 1956 the Billy Cotton Band Show had just transferred from radio on the BBC Light Programme to BBC TV and my landlady was puzzled that I could resist the new experience of watching it.

The first commercial test of a helicopter was in 1946. In 1947 it was used for the first time for the delivery of airmail in Los Angeles (see above).

1946

	Married women allowed to work in the Civil Service
	Family Holiday Camp opened, Somerset, Pontin's
	First radar contact with the moon
January	First meeting of UN General Assembly, London
February	Bank of England nationalised
	The *Jitterbug* dance swept Britain
	First commercial helicopter tested
March	**Churchill's *Iron Curtain* speech in USA**
	BBC Home Service radio broadcast Alistair Cooke's first *Letter from America* (the programme continued until 2004)
June	TV licenses introduced
	Bread rationing imposed
July	Clement Attlee (Labour) replaced Winston Churchill (wartime coalition) as Prime Minister
August	Family allowances introduced, paid to mothers
	Free milk for all pupils under 18 in state schools
September	British Communist Party organised mass squat of homeless families in empty London properties
	BBC radio Third Programme started
October	**Neurenberg trials of Nazi war criminals began**
	Dick Barton: Special Agent had its first daily episode on the BBC Light Programme
November	Slimbridge Wetland Reserve opened
	Stevenage designated as Britain's first new town to relieve overcrowding due to the London bombings

College return after war

Bessie Walshaw

In the last months of the war, I left home to start a degree course at King's College of Household and Social Science (KCHSS), part of London University. Because of the bombing in London it had been evacuated to Leicester University and they allowed us to use part of their premises. I lived in digs with a landlady who thought that, as I was from Yorkshire, I needed a good supply of cooked tripe, which was unrationed. It is true that tripe was one of my favourite dishes (and remains so), but simply as honeycomb tripe seasoned with vinegar and never cooked (it has already been boiled before sale). I endured it as graciously as I could.

At the time the Principal of Leicester University was the father of the now famous Attenborough brothers, who were about my age. I remember going carol singing with David and Richard. So did one of my college friends there, who later married one of them.

When I started at KCHSS I was required to take two additional courses. These were in chemistry and physics, subjects not then taught in girls' grammar schools, but felt necessary as a foundation for a science-based degree. KCHSS offered two main degree programmes, one intended to lead towards a career in teaching, the other to research into food and nutrition. I followed the teaching programme, as both my parents were teachers. The other programme seemed more interesting, as it was more scientific and included doing tests for the food industry, but it was my brother who had been thought to be the potential scientist in the family, and I followed my parents' choice, as was usual in those days.

Because food rationing was still in force, much of my food course was taught as theory rather than by practice. Despite not having much to do with actual cooking, we had to wear white hats of a special design with folded rims. Anything requiring meat as an ingredient was demonstrated by the tutor rather than undertaken by us students. We learnt the theory of wines but never tasted them.

Two flat irons, always used with a cloth round the handle as this got hot as well as the ironing surface. It was usual to have two irons, so that one could be heating on the fire while the other was in use.

Practical work was limited to simpler methods, such as how to heat flat irons on a fire and spit on them to test when they were hot enough to iron shirts. Removing stains from fabric loomed large on the syllabus – perhaps it was because it involved careful husbandry and didn't involve spending much money.

For my last year we moved back to Notting Hill in London, where I stayed in the University Hall of Residence. I made new friends, but rarely went out to enjoy what London had to offer as we had our heads down for our final exams.

After graduating I did a postgraduate year in London leading to a teaching diploma. At the college there I remember a security exercise in which we had to be lowered down on ropes as though being rescued from a fire. No one else volunteered so I was the first to do it. I got stuck half way down and was left hanging for what seemed a long time while more apparatus was brought. I hope I was wearing trousers, but it was more common then for girls always to wear skirts.

Refugee doctor

Robert Weiner

My family arrived in Britain on 1st June 1939, Jewish refugees from Prague. After three months in London and by complete chance, my Mum and I came to spend the duration of the war in Torquay (how that happened is a story which I told in Newcastle U3A's book *The Snoring of a Thousand Men: Tales of wartime childhoods*). We lived off charity for 18 months but then several changes in the law meant that my Dad was allowed to work, initially as a science teacher in a school, but eventually in his profession as a doctor. He joined the Royal Army Medical Corps (RAMC), serving in West Africa and later on as a medical officer to a Royal Artillery unit in Warburg, Germany.

Robert with his father and mother in Torbay: 1945.

His turn for demobilisation came in 1946 and the question then arose 'What now?' Such news as they were able to get from Czechoslovakia suggested that if they returned they were likely to meet with a fairly unenthusiastic reception. In addition there was the matter of the university Dad had attended, because at the time when he went to medical school Prague had two Universities, one Czech and the other German. He had chosen to go to the German one and this was now severely frowned upon.

Dad's politics veered heavily to the left and his first thoughts were therefore to go to Russia. However (thank goodness) Mum had other ideas. Before marrying she had taught English for a while in Prague and now, after living in Britain for six years, she absolutely loved living here. What is more, although there was relatively little anti-Semitism in Czech society (compared, say, to Poland or Austria), my parents found Britain to be in a completely different league in this respect and I'm sure that was another major consideration.

And finally of course there was 'the boy' (me). I was seven years old when we arrived and now I was 14 and in the Third Form at Torquay Grammar School. I had gradually forgotten most of my Czech and starting up in a different education system would have meant quite an upheaval. So the decision was made to try and stay in Britain.

Fortunately for us the regulations regarding practising medicine were relaxed at the end of the war and the qualifications of refugee doctors like my Dad were accepted as valid. As his specialism was haematology, he applied for and got a post with the National Blood Transfusion Service in Birmingham. We moved to Birmingham in 1946 and my parents never saw Prague again.

I have been there since the Velvet Revolution in 1989 and was pleased to be able to show our three children something of our family's history.

In my view the best two decisions my Mum and Dad ever made were to get out of Prague in 1939 and to stay put in Britain in 1946.

After scarlet fever

Betty Dawson

In 1946 my brother caught scarlet fever and was rushed to the Fever Hospital in Buxton. Visiting was on Sunday afternoons, and once there we had to climb up a wooden staircase and speak to him through a window. My parents were so pleased when he got better, but brought him home only to find that they had a very red-bodied daughter. So the whole charade started again.

A comptometer was a key-driven mechanical calculator. It was very fast, as each key automatically added or subtracted as soon as it was pressed, and could respond simultaneously to a skilled operator using four fingers at the same time.

When I was 16 my parents decided I should be a comptometer operator, as they had heard it was a well-paid office job. So off to college I was sent. Parents in those days decided what was best for their children. I started work in an Electrical Engineering firm and was paid £2/10/- (£2.50) a week. My parents took £1 from this, and I paid for my food, fares and holidays with the rest. I remember that if you went abroad you were only allowed to take £25 out of the country.

When they first took sweets off the rationing (for four months) in 1949, I went into Woolworth's on my way to work and bought four Mars Bars. I have never eaten one since.

The door handle of a mid-century Woolworth's shop. This shop was up-to-date in being air conditioned, as shown on the right of the handle, but the last Woolworth's in Britain closed down in January 2009.

My brother at 18 enrolled in an Agricultural College, as we came from farming stock, but this had to be postponed as conscription to National Service for two years was compulsory at that age. He was lucky and spent most of his time in the RAF in Egypt. He enjoyed it, but many others were very unhappy about the experience.

For entertainment I belonged to a church-run Youth Club for 16-21 year olds. We went on long hikes, cycled to Warwick and went to see Shakespeare plays performed at Stratford–on-Avon, which was only 20 miles away. We even acted in Nativity Plays for the church. On Saturdays we had dances – wonderful!

Then I heard that Hall Green had a drama society and had got permission from the Council to build a theatre for themselves. The idea of bricklaying really got to me, and I joined. My jobs were mixing mortar, carrying bricks and at last actually laying the bricks. I learnt how to lay flooring and many other things.

When we completed it we joined the Little Theatre Organisation and put on four productions a year. I loved working back stage, although I had no nerve for acting, but enjoyed it all.

Clocking-in at work in the 1940s.

This machine, made by British Time Recorders Supply and Maintenance Company Ltd of Borough High Street, London SE1, was designed to ensure that a nightwatchman stayed awake. Every hour he had to pull the lever at the left which rang a bell and stamped the time on a paper roll.

The machinery inside the box (right) was kept locked, so as to ensure that the hands of the clock could only be changed by a person in authority.

58

1947

	Dead Sea Scrolls found
	Holograms invented by Gabor in Hungary
January	**One of the most severe winters on record**
	Coal mines nationalised
	British coins no longer made from silver
February	Polaroid instant camera demonstrated in New York
	Dior's New Look in women's clothes
March	**Peak in post-war births: the Baby Boomers**
	Widespread flooding as thaw came
April	**School leaving age raised to 15**
May	Cold War began: anti-communist Truman Doctrine
June	**Marshall Plan inaugurated American aid to Europe**
	Restrictions on foreign travel lifted
July	UFOs said to be seen in USA, especially at Rosswell where an 'alien' was rumoured
August	**India and Pakistan gained independence from Britain**
	Mining accident in Whitehaven killed 104
	First experimental reactor in Western Europe opened at Harwell
	First Edinburgh Festival of the Arts
	Thor Heyerdahl's raft Kon Tiki reached Polynesia from South America, demonstrating the possibility of early migrations
October	**The sound barrier was broken by a Bell X-1 rocket plane**
November	**Princess Elizabeth married the Duke of Edinburgh, the first royal marriage to be**

	televised, although the ceremony within the Abbey was only broadcast on radio
	End of British Mandate for Palestine as UN approved Partition Plan into Arab and Jewish regions
	Contempt of USA Congress: 10 Hollywood actors refused to appear before the Un-American Activities Committee in Senator McCarthy's hunt for communists
December	First permanent Oxfam charity shop opened
	Norway started the tradition of giving a Christmas tree for Trafalgar Square
	The transistor was invented by Bell in the USA

New and old in 1947: the Bell X-1 rocket plane broke the sound barrier and the Kon-Tiki proved migration across the Pacific was possible.

Exams, exams – and bananas

Peter Jones

Gaining entrance to university is difficult for many students today. In 1947 the problems were different and even more complicated. After School Certificate (O-Levels) in 1945 I was told that I should stay at school in the sixth form to take Higher School Certificate (A-Levels) and think about going to university.

No one in my family had been to university and I thought it might be too expensive, but I was assured that there were now lots of scholarships and grants available that would pay, and the important thing was to study hard.

Applications for university entrance had to be made at the start of the second year in the sixth form and each university required a separate application. In some cases the application required a cash deposit, which was forfeit if a place was offered but not taken up. Some required entrance exams to be taken at school. I successfully took the Imperial College exams and was also offered entrance to another London college. Choosing London was a good idea because, if you took and passed four main subjects in the Higher School Certificate, you obtained an Inter BSc exemption and the university course was reduced from three years to two. I was well aware that, despite the grants, there would be stressful financial demands on my family.

By Christmas 1946 I thought things were settled. It was a terrible winter and we lived on a Pennine ridge almost 700 feet above sea level so that going to school for me was a trudge through deep snow for about half a mile. Remarkably most of the buses kept running, school was never closed and there were few absences.

We sat 'mock' exams in January, and then four of us sixth formers were summoned to the Headmaster to be told that we had been chosen to take the Oxford entrance scholarship exams in March. We were stunned. No one from the school had gone to Oxford (although the Head was an Oxford graduate) so we had no idea what was involved. It was just another set of exams – or so we thought.

The thaw started in March so, when Colin, Roger, John and I set off for Oxford, the train was running through deep floods (the good old steam engines) but was not seriously delayed. We settled in at Balliol College, overawed by the extraordinary buildings, and nervously awaited the exams. Apart from the usual grind of Maths, Chemistry and Physics we had a language paper with passages for translation into English – from French and Latin (which I could try) and from German and Greek (which meant nothing to me). There was also a general paper and several exhausting interviews. At the end of a week a list was put on the notice board saying who was to go home and who was to stay for another week of exams – mainly practical exams and interviews. We went home exhausted, but there was little time for rest – Higher School Certificate exams were looming in June.

After a few weeks John and I learned that we had been successful and had places at Balliol in the autumn of 1947. These are offers that you feel you can't refuse, although the Oxford Chemistry course was four years (as opposed to the two years in London with Inter exemption).

John had a special problem. At school he had been placed in a group studying German, whereas I studied Latin (I don't remember that there was ever any choice in the matter). At the time there was a requirement at Oxford (and some other universities including Durham) that, whatever the course you proposed to study, you must have obtained not merely a pass but a credit in Latin. After studying from March to June, John had (remarkably) obtained a pass – but that wasn't good enough. He re-took the exam in September and was allowed to start university in October. But when he obtained only a pass again he was forced to leave for a year. I thought then (and I still think) that was a cruel and unreasonable decision. John went back to school to continue studying Latin (successfully) and returned to Oxford in 1948.

He had also persuaded the Headmaster to allow him to go to the local Girls Grammar School to study Biology. Both schools and universities were remarkably rigid institutions in those days and Biology was regarded as quite a dangerous subject to expose adolescent boys to.

I hadn't quite finished with exams before starting university. I discovered that Oxford had a 'First Public Examination' – for which there was no teaching, but which was at a level a bit beyond Higher School Certificate, and which had to be passed some time during the first year. I think this was quite a nice little earner for the university since the fees were not trivial and the exams were held four times a year. I discovered that I could take these exams in September before starting my course so I climbed back on to the treadmill for the summer. With a sigh of relief when I passed these exams I 'matriculated' (ie officially became a student) in October 1947.

My chief memory of the first few weeks was feeling cold and hungry. The rooms that I shared with another student had a tiny coal fire for heating and, from time to time, we were provided with a small bucket of slaty coal which often decrepitated noisily when lit. My coal-miner father laughed when he heard of this and said that such coal might contain the odd detonator, which would be even noisier. I've never been quite sure whether he was joking.

Extra warm clothing was required but clothes rationing made that difficult to obtain. The solution was provided by the Army Surplus

Store, where I was delighted to get a very cheap, but very cosy, sheepskin waistcoat.

Food rationing was still severe in 1947. My ex-servicemen fellow students made much use of a nearby Indian Curry House to supplement the limited and often quite unappetising college food, but this was beyond the pockets of most of the young ex-Grammar School boys. Occasional food parcels from home helped but we also found a transport café near the car factory which sold cheap, nutritious, 'greasy spoon' grub. So, within a few weeks, survival strategies were in place and normal student life had started.

One evening in the dining hall, the Head Steward of the college walked down the length of the hall bearing a large, covered silver salver. He stopped when he came to my friend Neville and myself and, with a flourish, removed the cover to reveal four bananas - two for Neville and two for me. We were 'Blue Ration Book Boys', officially *children* because we were under eighteen and we were the only students in the college entitled to a ration of bananas.

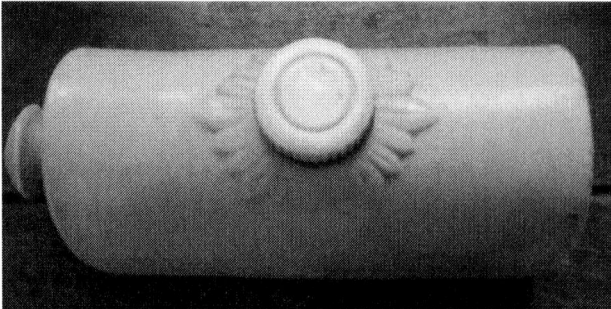

This earthenware bed-warmer could be filled with hot water to bring comfort to cold feet.

Milking French cows

Ruth Lesser

T he only other person in the compartment was a young soldier with his khaki kit-bag. I put my suitcase (no wheels on them in those days) on the netted rack over the seat. I was trying to subdue my excitement. My parents had seen me onto the train at Forster Square station, Bradford, and it was the first time I had had to travel so far and on my own. I was going, age 16, to France to stay on a farm.

It was the summer of 1947 and the War had been over for two years. Peace had allowed my school to invite a French *assistante* to come to help the girls who were doing French for their Higher School Certificate (the equivalent of today's A-levels). '*Assistante*', my father, a French teacher himself, reminded me meant someone who was *present* not necessarily assisting. But Mademoiselle in this case was very helpful. She had a friend who was a farmer's wife and who was willing to take a pupil for the summer holidays so that she could improve her knowledge of English. I was the lucky chosen one. My mother's reaction was 'A farm! There'll be plenty to eat': we were still feeling the pinch with food rationing. My father felt I had enough French to cope.

So they said farewell to me as they put me on the train to London, (the trains were powered by steam and had carriages partitioned into compartments and doors you had to open from outside by

A steam train with compartments, still running today on the Devon coast.

leaning out of the window). I had tickets to get me to the ferry to cross from Dover, a hotel booked in Paris for the night and a ticket to Thouars in the centre west of France.

Except that in this case the train was not going towards London, but towards Edinburgh. In those days stations had no electronic signs for departures and arrivals: the system was to ask a porter. It was when we got to the first station and I realised that we were going north not south that the situation began to worry me. The young soldier in my compartment had been similarly misled, and we both decided to get out and check with someone on the platform where the train was going. It did seem to be Edinburgh.

We had quite a long wait for a train which *was* going to London. I don't remember whether I shared my sandwiches with my fellow stray; I hope I did. It was getting dark when we arrived at King's Cross. The soldier had arranged to stay the night at a YMCA hostel, and I accompanied him there. The burly official at the door turned me away sharply when I asked if they could find a bed for me there, too. No females at the Young *Men's* Christian Association hostel!

Fortunately my father had taken me sometime before on a trip to London to go to the British Museum. It was on that occasion that I had literally bumped into the two Royal Princesses, Elizabeth and Margaret Rose, when I dashed across an aisle between cabinets of models of Saxon villages to tell my father what I had seen. He was white-faced and standing rigidly to attention as the royal party was interrupted in their crossing aisle by the exuberant schoolgirl. It must have marred the royal educational visit, but there were no comebacks.

Now in my current emergency on the way to France I remembered that we had stayed at the Church Army Hostel, and that it wasn't too far from King's Cross. The YMCA doorkeeper gave me directions, and the CAH did find me a cubicle. It was an uncomfortable night. I was daunted by the crude conversations in the common room, hungry, and worried about the safety of my luggage. I also had the problem of my travel bookings all now being a day late. I think breakfast must have been included in the deal and I got away as soon as I could.

I found that the ferry at Dover could still take me when I explained what had happened. So in fact could the Paris hotel near the Gare du Nord, but my negotiations this time had to be in French. I also managed to send a telegram (no mobiles then) from the hotel to my hosts on the farm warning them I would be arriving a day late. (I decided not to send one to my parents until I got to my destination, as I knew they would feel worried and perhaps abashed). The hotel had lush dark red carpeting. My room was on the first floor, and like most hotel rooms then did not have en suite facilities. I was being followed by a man who was attempting to engage me in conversation and who hovered at my door, which I quickly closed on him. I waited, listening to my heart beat, for him to go away, as I needed to find the bathroom. I had to wait a long time without hearing receding footsteps and eventually opened the door: he had gone. Was his creeping away silently just the plush carpet or a retaliation for the rejection?

I had a morning to spend before catching a train going south to Thouars and decided to visit the cathedral of Nôtre Dame. Here, too, I had an experience of how alluring French men found sixteen year-old girls on their own. Climbing up the spiral staircase in the tower I felt a hand behind me. I turned round with what I hoped was an icy face and an appropriate reaction in improvised French: '*Vous voulez passer, Monsieur*'? and it worked. He retreated down the stairs.

My host, Mme C, met me at Thouars station, and turned out to be a likeable, stylish woman. We had quite a walk to the farmhouse. Mme carried my suitcase on her bicycle and we walked along the edges of fields of maize with the cicadas beginning to sing in the delicious warmth of early evening. The farmhouse was a two-storey building set in a sun-bleached garden, and consisted of an upper and lower room on each side of the central door. The sanitation consisted of an earth closet at the end of the back garden in an unsubstantial wooden hut with many gaps in its walls. Five-year-old Jean-Mi took great delight in peeping through them when I used it, and I learnt to time my visits to when he was otherwise engaged. It was also necessary to check for spiders, frogs and other creatures. The house surprisingly had a telephone (more than we had then in England), which was on a shared line. One night it was put out of action by a violent storm, and there was relief that the lightning had not set fire to the house itself.

M and Mme C were generous and hospitable. Mme was a teacher – hence her wish to improve her English – but had a *crise de foie* (liver trouble) and was happy for me to improve my French instead. I spent most of my time helping Monsieur C, Fernand, with the farm tasks. I learnt how to milk cows (by hand of course), something that held me in good stead when we later kept our own goats in Nottinghamshire. There is a skill and peaceful comradeship in milking when you get to know the animals; it is a shared, measured activity and there is no point in hurrying. I also learned how to yoke the two oxen that were used for heavy haulage.

The maize had ripened and days were spent scything the crop and loading them onto the cart. I recall a rather winsome, innocent episode when Fernand and I were sitting among the maize eating our baguette and cheese chunks at a break in the work when he quizzed me on the meanings of '*Je t'aime*' and *Je t'aime bien*'.

One day the massive threshing machine arrived which went round several farms and all the farmers travelled round with it to help each other. There was a gory tale about how a young man had been caught in the machine and I was warned to keep well out of its reach. The day it arrived meant that Mme C had to provide a large meal for all the workers, and as usual we ate on tables put together in the front garden under the trees. The food was always excellent. My favourite was the potato and onion soup with large

68

chunks of baguette floating in it. I got accustomed to the French style of having the ingredients of the meal served one at a time. The bottles of local wine were endless (in September I helped with the grape treading). Chickens (a rare treat in Britain then) and eggs were in good supply.

My hosts did their best to show me more of French life. Mme and I made a trip to Paris to a fashion show of haute couture. It was just the time when the New Look had been introduced by Dior and the fashion presentation was at one of the big Paris houses (I can't now remember which). By a fluke I was the owner of a New Look coat, with a pinched waist and calf-length flared skirt. My mother had bought it for me with an unexpected windfall. She had handed in at the police station a wallet she had found and which hadn't been reclaimed within the six month limit and she had therefore been allowed to keep. Mme C must have been under the impression that I had an up-to-date knowledge of fashion, and particularly asked me to wear the coat in the audience at the show.

A New Look coat advertised in the magazine Home Notes, 1951.

The family also had a week's holiday at the seaside resort of Les Sables d'Olonne and took me with them. Here again fashion came into play, this time in hairstyles. A stylist was putting on stage in a theatre a display of different hairstyles using live models, who put their heads through oval frames in the scenery. One of the models hadn't turned up, and I became Mlle X. Not only was my hair teased into an elaborate style, but I was heavily made up – a complete novelty for me, coming from a home where even lipstick was considered brazen and shamefully dishonest.

My visit came to an end to my great regret. I had overstayed the school holidays and had to return after six weeks. It was an enriching experience, and surprising in its way, now I look back, with how much freedom I had. My parents were happy to see me back safely, but my mother's first thought was to get me in the bath; she thought I had brought back too much of the farm with me. I have no photographs of my French visit to illustrate my account: I didn't get my first camera until 1956 (and then photographs were in black and white until colour film became available at a manageable price in the 1970s).

The visit must have helped me with my Higher School Certificate exams in French, and I did well enough to be awarded a State Scholarship to go to university with fees and maintenance paid. The grant was good enough to be able to enjoy living in London without scrimping.

It was an amazing time to be at university, especially for a provincial girl. Women were a small minority in universities then and many of the places were taken by young men who had completed their national service and been awarded government grants. For women the choice of potential partners (in those days when virginity was prized, and babies out of wedlock were scandalous, partners would usually become spouses) was vast. Many of the men were three years older than the women students, and I revelled in what seemed to me to be a sophisticated and exciting world.

Sharing a tiny flat with a girl student in my final year was the ultimate in feeling I was running my own life. It was in Mornington Crescent (yes!) and our windows faced the Craven-A cigarettes office quarter which had replaced the garden in the middle of the crescent, and which

was emblazened with a vast hoarding claiming that 'Craven-A will not affect your throat'. It was not till 1957 that it was recognised that smoking cigarettes such as Craven-A caused cancer.

Another experience I had a couple of years later in 1952 was also entirely dissonant with today's lives. Newly married, I left the delights and strains of London for Nottingham where my husband had been offered an editorial job. As a graduate and trained advertising copywriter from a big London agency, which had just launched the new washing powder *Surf*, I arrogantly assumed I would find it easy to get a post in Nottingham. Not so. At an interview at a well-known large pharmaceutical company there, I was told in so many words to go away and have a baby, as they did not consider as employable young women who were recently married.

Today, of course, such a blatant dismissal would be against the law.

Life as a country doctor's son

Derry MacMahon

Towards the end of the war in Europe, my parents, with reasonable foresight, gave notice to the boarding school, which my brother and I attended. So we were to live at home again. Compared with this, distant Japan (still at war) meant very little to me. So far as I knew then I had no connection with the Far East, but I was soon to learn some things which had a bearing on events there.

Home had changed from what I remembered before the war. To begin with we no longer had someone who was a living-in maid. My father, a country doctor who ran his practice single-handed, had needed someone capable of dealing with requests for house calls and the telephone. She naturally had been paid more than a domestic servant This was something which upset other ladies who had maids and who accused my mother of spoiling their sources of cheap labour. Now a woman was employed to clean the surgery and dispensary, but it was my mother who had to deal with calls from patients, and this meant that we could not do as much as a family as in the past.

My mother, the daughter of a local farmer, was very aware of her position as the Doctor's Wife, so held herself aloof from social activities in the village and would not allow us children to associate with the local children, thus causing us often to be lonely.

So far as daily living went there was little change. Rationing became more stringent, but this had little or no effect on me. I was never hungry, thanks to the generosity of farmer patients and their wives. Also there was a healthy barter system which had existed during the war. For example, one family bred rabbits and would swap two of them for a chicken. We always had a good supply of sugar because it was never put on the table. So there was always some which could be exchanged for tea, as often people who came to the house, for example as private patients, had to be offered hospitality.

My father's hobby was his horses. We usually had two and a pony, so he bought two small fields with out-buildings for stables. One of these became a pig-sty in which there were usually two occupants. A licence had to be obtained before a pig could be killed. What often happened was that two were killed when a licence for one slaughter was issued. There was a story, probably apocryphal, that a policeman, visiting a farm to check that all was as it should be, saw sides of bacon and hams hanging from the kitchen ceiling. He observed that they had killed a pig and was assured that all had been done according to regulations. In reply he commented that it must have been the only pig in creation that had three hind legs. He left with a bulky parcel under his arm.

To eke out the petrol ration my parents bought a smart gig. Quite a number of people had also done this. It meant that a pleasant drive could be taken in the country lanes and in fact we used to take trips to the seaside in it. Some hotels still offered ostler services so there could be pleasant afternoon outings without having to worry about the pony. My father took to using the gig for his home visits, and could often do them in less time than if he used the car, as he could excuse himself on account of his slow transport.

One evening on going into one of our fields my brother and I came across two children and a Chinese lady, Nellie Chen, playing a ball game. Although they invited us to join them we were too shy to do so. We told our mother of this, and learned that the children's father was Leonard Wilson, Bishop of Singapore, who had been captured and tortured by the Japanese, who accused him and Nellie Chen of spying. (He had been able to get his wife and children out of Singapore before the Japanese occupation.) They were now reunited and staying with his mother who lived locally. This meant that we could have some company of our own age and get to know a truly wonderful man, who had brought his supposed accomplice to this country so that she could have the best medical care. Some years later, when he had become Bishop of Manchester, while doing confirmations he looked down the line of people awaiting him, and saw one of his former prison camp guards. After the ceremony he asked the man what had made him become a Christian and was told that it was his exemplary behaviour while under hardship that had first put the thought into his head.

The school I attended was private and probably expensive. The headmaster was a man born after his time, and would have been more at home in Victorian days. His chief target was to get his charges through the Common Entrance Examination, so that they were eligible for entrance to public school. Consequently my slight knowledge of the war went to the back of my mind. I tried to behave in the urban manner of my school fellows, but my background was rural and was generally thought to be unpolished.

In 1947, the year of a very severe winter, I came more into my own. The Wilsons, my brother and I used to catch a bus at ten past eight, and normally we would arrive at school at about nine o'clock. Because of the bad state of the roads the bus was often late and due to further delays we often walked the last two or three miles, arriving at school after ten o'clock. To get home by half past five we would leave school at half past three. Despite this dreadful weather the only hardship I felt was the shortage of coal, which was used for cooking as well as heating. It is amazing how much old wood can be found and I found chopping and sawing it was fun.

My father's routine was also affected badly by the weather. The snow was so deep that it was impossible to use the car. So the horses came into their own. His two became so exhausted that he had to borrow two more, thus giving each animal three days rest, while he made his calls every day.

I remember his anger one day, when after getting home in the middle of the afternoon for his lunch, the telephone rang and he had to set out to see a man in a village about four miles away. Having saddled up a fresh horse, off he went, and on arrival saw a man standing outside his house. He asked the man to keep an eye on the horse, only to be told that he was the patient and had a 'bit of a headache'.

This was just before the time when the National Health Service came in to existence, bringing with it changes in demands on my father's time. He then found it necessary to employ an assistant in the surgery. The number of people wanting to consult him increased because everything was free. He could no longer maintain the horses to the exacting standard he desired, so they were sold, and because we lived more than seven miles from the nearest town he had to do a great deal of dispensing. Needless to say the amount of paper work increased immediately.

When the time came for me to prepare for the Common Entrance Examination my headmaster decided that public school was not for me because of my impaired vision and did not allow me to go into higher classes for two years. My parents had a meeting with him, hoping for some constructive advice, but all he said was that I should be sent to the local blind school. So they enquired about the syllabus there and were told that I would be taught Braille, basketry and rush work. If I showed the correct aptitude, I might be trained as a piano tuner. My father especially refused to consider this idea. After exhaustive searches a small independent grammar school was found, where I was eventually happy.

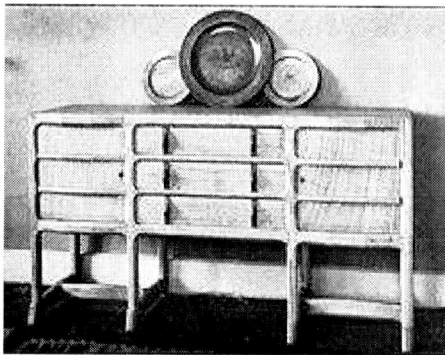

*This oak dresser is an example of Utility
Furniture, aimed at economy of materials
and designed by Gordon Russell, director of
the Council of Industrial Design in 1947.
The scheme ended in 1952.*

XIVTH OLYMPIAD

LONDON

1948

1948

	Beginning of the Berlin Airlift against the Russian Blockade
	Communist guerrilla insurgency in Malaya, prior to independence from Britain (achieved in 1957)
	The first Kinsey Report, on men's sexual behaviour
	South Africa imposed *apartheid*
	'Prefabs' constructed to help overcome the housing shortage
	1930s game of *Lexico* was upgraded to *Scrabble*
	Abolition of plural voting in parliamentary elections, which had allowed university graduates and property owners a second (or even third) vote
	Velcro was invented
January	**British Railways nationalised**
	Mahatma Gandhi assassinated in India
February	Communists invaded Czechoslovakia
March	Britain signed the Treaty of Brussels with Benelux countries
April	**UN established World Health Organisation**
May	Poor Law superseded by the National Assistance Act
	State of Israel came into being
June	First female Vice Chancellor of a British University (Professor Lilian Penson at London)
	First Aldeburgh Festival
	World's first stored-program computer at Manchester (SSEM)
	500 Jamaican immigrants arrived on the *Empire Windrush*

July	**Olympic Games in London, July-August**
	Town and Country Act requiring permission for land development and listing buildings
	National Heath Service began
	Children's Act transferred responsibility to local government Children's Departments
	First chapter of Alcoholics Anonymous
	End of bread rationing
	Gas Boards created
	USA ended racial segregation in its armed forces
September	**First comprehensive schools**
	Birching and flogging abolished
October	First postwar Motor Show introduced the Morris Minor and Land Rover and 13 other new models to 562,954 visitors
	USSR launched a space missile
November	Princess Elizabeth gave birth to a son, heir to the throne
	First broadcast of *Any Questions* (BBC Home Service)
December	**UN Assembly adopted a Universal Declaration of Human Rights**

1948: Morris Minor.

France and Franco's border guards

Hilary Sigmund

In 1948 my parents decided we would have a holiday in France. We had a heavy old Ford V8 Pilot car which was loaded onto the cross-channel ferry by a hoist (*see photo*).

There were five of us, my parents, sister Margie, 16, brother Jim, 9, and myself, 13. The war had been over for about three years but there was still strict austerity in Britain and a trip to the continent – although commonplace now – was then distinctly adventurous.

1948: hoisting the car onto the French ferry at Dover. Drive-on ferries at Dover and Calais were not introduced till 1953.

Our route took us through Limoges to astonishing Carcassone. With eyes popping we drove up to the old city through the narrow streets and arched gateway right into the heart of the close built medieval city where we were to stay. Nowadays I am sure this is all a strictly pedestrian area.

The French gave us a huge, warm welcome embracing us as allies wherever we went and calling us *sympathiques*. Once when we stopped to watch grapes being harvested the pickers came across the fields, insisting on loading great bunches of grapes as gifts into our car boot. The boot was nearly filled and we ate the mouth-watering fresh fruit until we could eat no more. For our lunches we would stop and buy delicious fresh bread and cheese. For our evening meal we nearly always chose *omelette aux fines herbes* as my father said this was the most delicious food in all France. He had a great deal of charisma but with hindsight he may have been putting a good spin on the cheapest course on the menu as at that time there was a strict limit (I think £5) on the amount of foreign currency Britons were allowed.

Then to Port Vendres and a day trip to the beach in Northern Spain. There we were questioned by a group of Franco's border guards – ill shaven, bored and heavily armed. One of them tried to make a pass at my sister but was disconcerted by a loud bang from a bottle opening, not from gunshot as he initially seemed to think. Not at all like our own dear police.

We stopped a night in Paris on the way home and went out to a restaurant called *l'Ecossais* with a band and singing.. It was called a *Boite de Nuit* but I can't imagine it was as dashing as the name suggests. Jim wore his kilt for a good deal of the trip and, as we walked in, the band miraculously launched into 'Annie Laurie'. For souvenirs Margie and I bought a *broderie anglaise* blouse each which I considered very fashionable. In those days we were spared the modern curse of the ubiquitous gift shop so the blouses were all we bought, though perhaps we had no more money anyway.

My older brother did not come with us as he was in Palestine doing National Service, remembered fondly for the luxury goods such as fruit cakes, canned pineapple and sweets which he could buy there and post home to us in Scotland still under rationing.

The strange thing is that at the time all this was exciting but to be expected, but recalling it now it is like another world.

I chose the Guides

Joan Hodgson

When I was eleven, I moved from a Newcastle primary school to an independent grammar school, having won a City Council scholarship which paid all the fees. Two years later a seven day timetable was introduced at the school. It caused quite a stir. It did not mean that we went to school seven days a week, but it was quite taxing working out which timetable day it was. The days, instead of being Monday to Friday were labelled 1 to 7, the first day of a new term being Day 1. If that was a Wednesday, say, the Friday was Day 3 and the following Monday Day 4 and so on.

Day 7 (Thursday of the second week) included a free activities afternoon. Some of us considered the inconvenience of the new system to be worthwhile because of the group activities every seventh afternoon. Most of these group activities cut right across the age range. The first one I joined was 'Exploring Newcastle'. We went to places such as the Castle Keep, the Law Courts and the Central Police Station.

After a few terms one of the options was to become a member of a new school Guide Company, which I chose with enthusiasm. At that time (1948) clothes were still rationed and uniform blouses were not available. An ex-army white nylon parachute was obtained and we spent hours in the school library during lunch breaks unpicking the seams of this huge round object. The Domestic Science (cookery and needlework) teacher dyed the pieces Guide blue and cut out all our blouses. We took the pieces home and our mothers machined them together. Navy berets were available without clothes coupons (hats had not required coupons throughout the war) and a leather belt and our navy school skirt completed our uniform. After a while the Guide Company became an after-school activity. At sixteen I moved on to the local Ranger Unit of which I was still a member at the time of the Coronation in 1953.

Knitted Guide and Scout toys from a 1950s pattern.

We lived in a semi - detached house, built pre-war, which like most houses of that era had two reception rooms. These were a dining room (which was really a living room in our case) and a sitting room which contained the three-piece suite, and where a coal fire was only lit on Sundays and special occasions.

My father was a radio engineer and in his spare time over many weeks he had been making a television set. Almost no-one had such a thing in those days, so I was very popular when my parents invited all the Rangers to our house to see the Coronation on our nine-inch cathode-ray tube TV screen. The TV had to be in the sitting room where there was room for it. I don't remember how we crammed everyone in so that they could all see the little screen. We managed and the occasion was enjoyed by all present.

We did not watch much television in those days as there was only one channel which broadcast programmes for only a few hours in the evening, but we listened to the wireless (radio) in the other room instead.

Working in a bank

Moira Tushingham

In 1948 at the age of 16 I started working for a large
commercial bank. They had recently mechanised their
accounting systems in the larger branches and were training
girls to operate the new machines. Two girls from my school were
employed to do this in Newcastle branches. Each branch had a
large number of young people working there so there was the
opportunity to make new friends and arrange social outings.

I was appointed as junior clerk in the small Gateshead branch
where there were seven or eight members of staff of varying ages.
The only mechanical equipment we had was an old typewriter that
the secretary was reluctant to let anyone else touch and a
rudimentary adding machine. This worked by pressing keys and
pulling a handle for each item to make a running total. I was pretty
quick at mental arithmetic so rarely used the machine. Every
column of figures was double-checked and even now I always
count a column from bottom to top and top to bottom.
Statements and ledgers were hand-written so I had to tidy up my
writing and alignment of figures. Standards were strict so, if a
statement looked messy, the whole thing had to be rewritten
before it was given to the customer.

Only large businesses had printed cheque-books. Private
customers did not have their names printed on cheques and it
could be difficult to decipher the scribbles they used as signatures.
This could lead to a cheque being entered on the wrong account
but as the signature was seen by three different people the error

An old typewriter with jammed letter bars, showing why the secretary at Moira's bank might have been reluctant to let junior staff use her machine.

was usually discovered before any real harm was done. Ball-point pens were available but we were not allowed to use them. The staff used fountain pens and I had to fill ink-wells on the customer's side of the counter every morning and make sure that the blotting pads were clean and tidy. My next job was to make everyone a cup of tea or coffee. It was a bit like being a monitor back in Junior School.

The opening hours were from 10am to 3pm from Monday to Friday and 10am to 12 noon on Saturdays. The staff started work at nine o'clock and no one was allowed to go home until the cash and books had been balanced to 1d. This made social life rather a problem as we never knew at what time we would be able to leave work. The only people in our street who had telephones were a doctor and a builder, so I couldn't even let Mother know if I was going to be late for tea. None of my friends had telephones either and mobile phones had not yet been invented.

One of my favourite jobs was to do the 'local clearing'. There were five banks in Gateshead, all within walking distance of one another. So every morning a junior clerk from each bank would take the cheques which had been paid in on the previous day and present

A new telephone of the 1950s with rotary dial.

them to the bank they had been drawn on. We each took it in turn to be the host bank so we would all meet at Barclays on Monday, Lloyds on Tuesday, Martins on Wednesday etc. It was good fun meeting up with other youngsters. One cold winter's day we decided that it would be much more congenial to meet in Carrick's café instead, but we found to our horror that some of our managers had got there first so we had to beat a hasty retreat. The benefit of local clearing was that cheques were cleared in 24 hours. Even cheques from other towns and cities were cleared in three days. They were sent to London each night, sorted next day and arrived at the relevant branch the following day. I cannot understand why sixty years later, with all the telecommunications equipment available, it takes banks five days to clear a cheque.

Staff uniforms had not yet been introduced so my outfit for the first few months was a skirt and jacket which my sister had worn for three years - a year while student teaching and two years at training college. Clothes were made to last and with a new blouse or hand-knitted jersey it still looked quite smart. Mother was quite generous in allowing me to keep all of my first month's salary of £9.10s.0d. Most of it was spent on a new winter coat. Nine pounds doesn't sound much after working for a full month but you could do quite a lot with it then.

Every Saturday night my friends and I would go dancing or sit in the cheaper seats in a theatre or cinema and we saved up to go away during our precious two weeks of holiday and sometimes during Bank Holiday weekends. We usually went walking, staying at Youth Hostels, but one year we decided to try to make some money by working on the land. It wasn't long after the war ended and farmers were short of staff so the government devised a scheme whereby you could stay in old army barracks and get paid for farm work.

We had to pay for the food that was provided and for our train fares all the way to Berkshire but we expected to make a profit. We had been told we would be picking plums but we didn't see any fruit trees, only fields full of potatoes. A sadistic Italian tractor driver raced up and down our field digging up a new row of spuds before we had even finished the last one so we got no chance to rest our weary backs. Half way through the following day the farmer arrived and was delighted to see our progress. We had picked so many potatoes that he could fulfil his contract for the week and he didn't need us to work anymore. Our group had let two Irishmen arrange terms of pay with the farmer as they said they had lots of experience in that field. They had foolishly agreed to us being paid by the hour. If we had been paid by piece (for each sack) we would have earned much more money. We could not find work the following day and were only offered a couple of hours on the following two days so the holiday was not a financial success.

I was quite content with banking until I was transferred to local head office (LHO) to work on the switchboard. The phones had to be manned from 9am until the senior staff locked up at night. This could be as late as 6pm. I was not expected to stay there until that time every night. There was a rota of machine operators who took it in turn to relieve me for a week each, to have lunch and coffee breaks and man the telephones for the last hour or so each day. The trouble was that no one supervised this arrangement and I never knew when the girls were going to turn up. In the evenings they would go downstairs to the cloakroom, put on fresh make-up, have a cup of coffee and chat to their friends. I am sure they used to save their filing jobs up for the week when they were supposed to be to be manning the switchboard, but the filing cabinets were out of earshot of the phone! If they didn't come to take over by 5pm I would go and seek them out to tell them that I was going home but it was rather annoying on days when most people had gone home by 4.30pm.

I soon realised when I first started working at LHO that I was the only member of the National Association of Bank Employees in that branch. Everyone else belonged to the Staff Association. Membership of this body was restricted to employees of our bank only and I couldn't see how its members could negotiate with the directors over pay and conditions when they relied on them for promotion. The National Union was open to clerks who worked in all banks and was affiliated to the Trades Union Council so I expected it to have more power. I was soon subjected to pep talks by several of the staff trying to persuade me to change my allegiance. As my work station was right next to the staircase I was a sitting duck as people had to pass me on their way to the cloakrooms and coffee room. The interruptions became so frequent that it amounted to harassment. It was difficult to think of anyone to complain to as my main protagonists were the assistant manager, the personnel officer and the manager's secretary. The manager was never seen in the banking hall. He worked in a remote room along a corridor. I hung around his office a few times in lunch breaks but was reluctant to knock on his door in case he was interviewing customers. I couldn't ask his secretary to make an appointment to see him as she would have told the others.

I am ashamed to say that I gave in, in the end, and joined their wretched Staff Association but I only paid one subscription to their funds. I took great delight in tearing up the standing order when I was transferred to another branch a few months later.

What followed were the happiest two years I spent working for the bank in a little four-man branch which was run by a manager, two six-foot-plus, rugby-playing hunks and me. The boys were full of fun and we teased each other mercilessly. We made so much noise laughing that the manager often had to come out of his office to restore calm. We made a good team, though, and often managed to leave work at 4pm every day. We usually went to the same dance hall on Saturday nights and I could always rely on them for a couple of dances from each.

My next appointment was as second cashier at the Chester-le-Street branch where I enjoyed working on the counter and getting to know the customers. Everything was fine until the cashier of the Birtley branch went on holiday. It had been the practice to send the second cashier to Birtley during this time but it was felt that it would be unsuitable for a young lady to run the branch on her own with just the help of a guard. It was decided to send the chief cashier to Birtley and I would take his place at Chester-le-Street.

Every Thursday the cash van paid us a visit. It brought the notes I had ordered to pay out weekly wages cheques the following day and took away bags of unwanted coins which had been paid into our branch by the local bus company.

When the van was unloaded at LHO it was discovered that a bag containing a hundred pounds of silver was missing. All hell was let loose and everyone seemed to be blaming me. We were late getting home that night as the manager and his assistant had to check all the cash in the branch and inspectors arrived next day to do a full audit. Fortunately for me I didn't worry too much as I was 100% sure that the loss of a hundred pounds of silver had nothing to do with me. I have always been a tidy packer and knew that ten bags of coins, in two rows, fitted on the cash trolley perfectly. I could visualise the seven white bags of silver, two green ones of nickel and one blue of copper in my mind's eye. I got so tired of telling this to the inspectors and LHO that I suggested that they sack me if I was wrong.

About a week later a hundred-pound bag of silver was found in a dark corner behind the strong room door of the Houghton-le-Spring branch. This was where the van had called before they came to us. I hope that their staff were chastised but I never got an apology for the trauma they had caused me. To make matters worse I was taken off the counter while they trained a younger male colleague so that he could go to Birtley when necessary instead of the chief cashier. I felt as if I had been demoted when I had to do his work on ledgers.

Soon after this I got engaged to be married so was too busy planning my wedding to worry much about work.

The bank paid females who got married what we girls called a 'dowry'. I had been working for them for over ten years so got the maximum amount of two hundred pounds. I think it was in lieu of pension, as women were not allowed to join the pension fund. Until 1959 the bank did not employ married women so I must have been one of the first to be allowed to stay. I had to write to LHO to ask permission, half hoping they would say 'no' as I fancied trying another kind of job. When they agreed I felt obliged to accept as the salary was too good to refuse.

Unfortunately I was transferred, once again, to LHO, so I was happy to retire from banking twelve months later.

I should like to think that banks recognise the value of women more now as they appoint them as managers and financial advisers and I hope that their internal complaints procedures have improved since my day.

The biggest difference in banking between then and now is the complete reversal of the official attitude towards debt which in those days was strongly discouraged. We now have credit cards and student loans and banks seem to encourage everyone to borrow money. I think the 'live now, pay later' attitude is a bad example to set the younger generations.

1949: The University of Manchester Mark 1 computer.

1949

	Legal Aid established
	Geneva Convention on treatment of prisoners
	Polaroid camera marketed
	East German Republic (DDR) proclaimed
	First commercial computer, the Ferranti Mk 1, based on a Manchester University model
	USSR tested an atomic bomb
	Children's books: Blyton's *Little Noddy Goes to Toytown* and Awdry's *Thomas the Tank Engine*
	Average price of a house in the UK was £1,911
January	Peacetime conscription regularised as *National Service*
	President Truman's *Fair Deal* to war damaged Europe
	Clothes rationing ended
March	Astronomer Fred Hoyle coined the term *Big Bang*
	Joe Louis, world heavyweight boxing champion, retired
	First round-the-world non-stop flight, by a B-50 Superfortress refuelled in flight
April	First private stately home opened to paying visitors, Longleat
	NATO created
	First women KCs (Rose Heilbron and Helena Normanton)
	Sweet rationing ended but was reinstated after four months due to shortages
	Ireland left the Commonwealth, but other republics joined (eg India)
May	EDSAC, the first practicable stored-program computer began to operate, Cambridge University

	First self-service launderette opened in London
June	Neptune's moon, Neried, discovered
	George Orwell published *1984*
	Dockers' strike forced government to call in troops to unload goods
September	**The pound was devalued by 30% against the US dollar**
	The Berlin Airlift ended
October	**People's Republic of China proclaimed**
	First luxury airliner, BOAC Speedbird Stratocruiser
December	First TV broadcasts outside London, transmitted to the Midlands from Sutton Coldfield

1949: the new Polaroid camera for instant photography.

Lend a hand on the land

Kathy Ellis

In 1949 food was still rationed and the government was concerned to increase home production. I remember hitch-hiking with my brother to Boston in Lincolnshire. We got a lift on a lorry to Pity Me in County Durham, and then to Lincolnshire, where we were met and taken to Spilsby. We were billeted in what I think was an ex-army camp. We were driven on a lorry to various farms in the area where we helped bring in the harvest. We were given a cooked breakfast every morning, a packed lunch to take out to the fields and dinner at night. I have a photo of myself ringing the bell for breakfast.

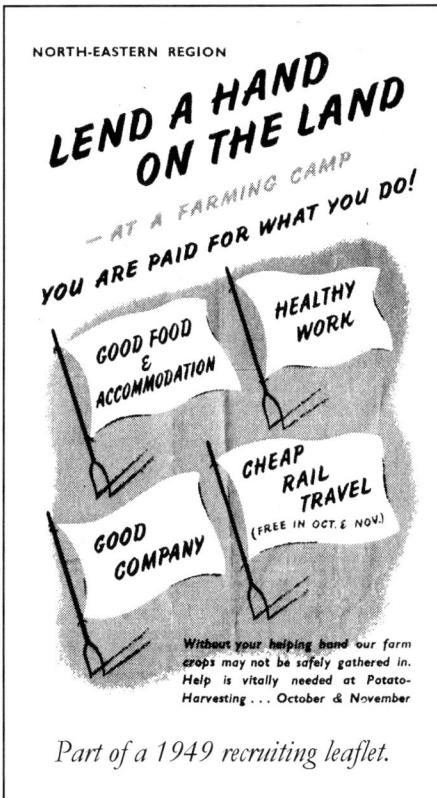

NORTH-EASTERN REGION

LEND A HAND ON THE LAND

— AT A FARMING CAMP

YOU ARE PAID FOR WHAT YOU DO!

GOOD FOOD & ACCOMMODATION

HEALTHY WORK

CHEAP RAIL TRAVEL (FREE IN OCT. & NOV.)

GOOD COMPANY

Without your helping hand our farm crops may not be safely gathered in. Help is vitally needed at Potato-Harvesting ... October & November

Part of a 1949 recruiting leaflet.

The Lend a Hand on the Land scheme paid people 1/6 (7½p) an hour to go to farm camps to help with weeding, planting, fruit picking etc. The charge for board and lodging was £1/10/- (£1.50) a week. In October and November for potato picking you were paid 1/9 an hour, the week's lodging was only 15/- (75p) and rail travel was free (but the job and the weather were worse!)

Luggage in advance

Kathleen Kurji

We always had an annual holiday; my father insisted on it and had a pound a week kept back from his wages to save up for it The first one I remember was 1949 or 1950. We went all the way to Beadnell. It may not have been far but we did it in style, sending a cabin trunk as advance luggage while we followed on the local bus. I don't recall any details, but there are photos of me playing happily on a sunny (!) beach, wearing a hand-knitted swimsuit.

Over the next few years times must have been harder because our holidays consisted of visits to relatives. Luckily they lived in Scotland, and always did their best to show us around. By 1958 things had improved again and we had a very exciting cruise to Orkney and Shetland. picking up the MV Gullfoss at Leith and spending five days on a round trip, stopping overnight at Kirkwall and Lerwick. My father was keen to show us where he had been stationed during the war. We enjoyed it so much we did it again the following year, but this time the sea was very rough and most of the passengers, and some of the crew, succumbed to seasickness crossing the Pentland Firth. I remember it as very beautiful in an understated way, and was

Kathleen on Beadnell beach in 1950 in a cotton two-piece.

thrilled to see seals basking on the beaches.

In the sixties like many others I tentatively tried package holidays. A rail trip to Yugoslavia is not to be recommended if you are looking for comfort (wooden benches pall after the first few hours) but we were intoxicated by the romance of it all - the names and the views, the unfamiliar food and of course the wine.

To me "The Boat Train" is still one of the most evocative phrases in the English language. Nowadays, of course, travel abroad is

Kathleen's father needed accommodation when he was demobbed, so took a job as a chauffeur to landed gentry in Northumberland; here he is with the stately Citroen he drove.

commonplace for many people, but I think our generation which was in at the beginning probably appreciates it all the more for the contrast with earlier experiences.

As well as memories of holidays, here are some of my early memories of school:
☐ The hated cushion we had to use for a nap every afternoon in Infants, and kicking it all the way home when it was no longer required.

☐ The shock at seeing my best teacher crying the day the King died.

☐ Morning assembly hymn 377, 'When a knight won his spurs'.

☐ Mental arithmetic tests.

☐ The pleasure of being read to at the last session on Friday, when I was 10.

☐ The belt.

☐ Scholarship day and the fateful envelope a few weeks later.

Kathleen and her family at Whitby in 1951.

1950

	World population 22,510,629,000
	First TV remote controls
	First pagers used
	Myxomatosis introduced into Australia to kill rabbits (introduced illegally to Britain in 1953)
	First human organ transplant, Illinois
January	BBC Radio (Light Programme) first broadcast *Listen with Mother*
	BBC TV showed a Test Card to help viewers adjust the screen before the programmes start, and showed a potter's wheel between programmes
February	First payment by a charge card (Diners Club) in New York
	Labour narrowly won the General Election giving Attlee a second term as Prime Minister
March	**Egypt demanded removal of British troops from Suez canal**
April	*Eagle* comic launched, featuring Dan Dare
	Corby in Northamptonshire was designated as the first New Town in Central England
May	First *Grand Prix* at Silverstone
	First package air holiday, by Horizon Holidays from Gatwick to Corsica for camping
	Motor fuel rationing ended after 11 years
June	**North Korea invaded South Korea, and the Korean War began**
	First (pilot) broadcast on BBC Radio of *The Archers* (still running today)
July	Sainsbury's opened the first purpose-built supermarket, Croydon
August	Britain sent 4000 troops to Korea
	BBC made its first TV broadcast from Europe

	Princess Elizabeth gave birth to a daughter
	Florence Chadwick swam the Channel in 13 hours 22 minutes
September	**Soap rationing ended**
	116 trapped miners in a Scottish colliery rescued
October	The Festival Ballet (English National Ballet) gave its first performance
	Re-built House of Commons first used
	Alan Turings's paper *Computing machinery and intelligence* was published
November	The first gay-lib association, LA, USA
	The Colombo Plan for economic development of S and SE Asia
December	The Stone of Scone was stolen form Westminster by Scottish Nationalists
	England's first National Park, the Peak District, was established

1950: TV test card, shown when the set was switched on, to allow the picture to be adjusted. TV sets had knobs at the front to adjust sound, brilliance etc. Sophisticated remote controls were not developed until 1970.

My 1950 shopping list

Kathy Ellis

When I was married in 1950 rationing was still on. Someone from the Co-op used to come every week and take my order, to be delivered later in the week. When we paid we were given a 'cheque' (see sample below). Twice a year we collected our dividend. The list here shows 5oz bacon 10d, ¼ stone of potatoes 5d, evaporated milk 1/-, a large white loaf 5½d, meat pasty 10 ½d, 2oz cheese 2d, ¼lb butter 6d, 1lb carrotts (sic) 2d, ½lb margarine 5d, 2lb onions 9d, 3lbs self-raising flour 1/0 ½.

Today's equivalent of 1/- (a shilling) is 5p; 5d would be about 2p today.

Houses and homes

Marjorie De'Ath

My grand parents and their five children, my father being the youngest, moved into a five-roomed terrace cottage in 1911, no longer able to afford the rent for their more spacious four-bedroom house. I was born in this house in 1940 and it was to this house, then rented by my Auntie, that Mum, Dad and I returned when Dad finally came home in 1945. We lived there until 1950.

Little had changed structurally in the house between 1911 and 1950. From the outside it looks much the same today. It is not in a charming terrace of stone country cottages, but of red brick, built with workers rather than managers in mind. In a big town the house would perhaps be undesirably basic, but it was on the edge of a small market town with a pleasant, grassy, banked river in front and a good garden behind. From the pavement the front door led into the front room. The back room was the living room, and between them the stairs went up to two bedrooms. The back of the house was three storeys, and from the living room a steep ladder staircase went down to the cellar, defying all modern health and safety rules. Outside wooden stairs went down from the living-room to the garden and stone steps went up from the cellar. Dad made wooden stair gates for all these to stop my brother crawling to his death. About ten yards down the garden was the toilet.

This was by no means the home for a hero, but people lived in far worse circumstances, and in some ways it was an improvement on our wartime living arrangements. It was near the town, had electricity and a flush toilet and we had children to play with. For entertainment value it was next not only to a railway line but to a level crossing and signal box, with a regular procession of passenger and goods trains drawn by large black steam engines. We would hurry to the back steps and wave to the engine driver.

1949: Brother David waving at the trains.

It was quite usual to have at least three or more generations in one house, but by 1945 there were no grandparents to join us. My parents rented their own house before the war, but it no doubt seemed sensible, now that Auntie was alone, for us to join her. Maybe there was no alternative. During the war at my grandfather's we were a household of seven, so this was still a downsizing even after my brother was born in 1947. Later we moved up the council waiting list as, with a boy and a girl, we qualified for one of the new three-bedroomed council houses being built. Meanwhile we all lived happily together.

Some things haven't changed as much as others: this is part of a newspaper advertisement for Campbell's soup in 1953; the can and emphasis on fresh vegetables are the same as today.

The back living-room was the heart of the house and the only room in winter to have any heating. There was a black-leaded fire-place with the fire basket in the centre, a small boiler with a tap to one side and a small oven the other. Both were heated by altering the setting of the damper. We cooked in the kitchen downstairs, but here we could boil a kettle or keep food hot or warm plates in the oven and egg shells could be dried to add to the chickens' food. The coal fire, our only heating, had to be cleaned out,

101

re-laid and lit every day, causing a good deal of dust. The ashes were riddled in a large sieve and the large cinders used on the paths in the vegetable garden (very uncomfortable if you fell over) while the ash was added to the compost heap. Periodically the chimney was swept to avoid the soot catching fire in it. The sweep also caused an amount of black dust as he brought the soot down the chimney and collected it in a large sheet. I remember how the furniture had to be covered and the carpet rolled back before he came. My job was to run down the garden to see the brush come out of the chimney pot, to prove the whole chimney was being swept.

The mantelpiece was wooden and high with a silky fringe tacked round to finish it off. The tiled hearth had a fender to keep coals from falling on the rug, which was a handmade proggy mat made from old coats. This was one of the tasks I could help with. The material was cut into strips of the same length and, with a sharp tool, fixed with a push-down and a pull-through to a piece of strong sacking in a random pattern. This was not art, just necessity. The main floor-covering was lino and a large coconut mat, hard-wearing but very scratchy to bare knees.

1945: Marjorie and her Mum beside the railway fence.

In front of the window was a gate-legged table where we ate all our meals. It folded out of the way as the room was small for three adults and two children. There was a sideboard with drawers for the things we needed for meals, the contents jangling when anyone moved too heavily across the room. There were four dining chairs, three easy chairs and a small seat for me. On a shelf was our only piece of technology: the wireless. Below it Dad made me my own personal space, a little cupboard where I kept my books and pencils, my pocket money and my sweets. No room for a television and computer in there!

The winter evenings would find us all in this room. Dad would read the paper or his library book, or perhaps mend something small. Mum and Auntie would read or knit and sew, as much of our clothing was hand made, and I would read or colour in a book, or draw, or cut out pictures to stick in a book. I could also help with the wool. It was bought in long continuous skeins and I would sit with arms outstretched, hands in each end of the skein while Auntie wound the wool into balls. Effort was put into teaching me to knit, but I was not really interested and no one insisted. A friend told me how much she enjoyed doing embroidery with her mother. I can remember being inwardly amazed: not my sort of thing. Someone would read me a story, or I would read to them. We might play Snakes and Ladders or Ludo or Dominoes or a card game. Or I would amuse my baby brother.

And we would listen to the wireless. I remember a show with Wilfred Pickles and Mabel-at-the-Table and Barney giving contestants their money; Much Binding in the Marsh, a comedy show with Kenneth Horne; Dick Barton Special Agent; Journey into Space; and Life with the Lyons. We all found these programmes, which today would seem so old-fashioned and unexciting, completely absorbing. There was a lot of light music. I was particularly taken with Donald Pears, a singer, but found him disappointingly plump and boring when we saw him on the stage at Skegness. The baby had his bath before the fire, and I helped to put him to bed. I had cereal and cocoa for my supper and then joined my brother in our bedroom.

The front room was the 'best' room. There was no rule of Keep Out, but it was not heated on ordinary days. On Sunday, at Christmas or other special times, the fire was lit and we all spent time sitting comfortably on the three-piece suite. I associate these times with wearing less comfortable best clothes. This was where visitors were entertained, but we had very few. My parents at this time had little social life apart from the extended family. Some came to stay, but others just came for the day, or my farming relations popped in between Sunday midday dinner and evening milking time. Mum didn't have friends in for coffee or tea and they never socialised with the parents of my school friends.

Here the fire-place was a normal, tiled one with a smart brass 'companion set' consisting of a poker, tongs for adding coal, a brush and a little shovel, all for attending to the fire. If you have never had a coal fire you have missed the pleasures of poking it and getting a blaze or adding extra coal, and of simply sitting looking at the flames, and the red caverns made between the glowing coals. The coal was brought into the house from the coal-house down the garden in a large 'brass' coal scuttle; not a job for me this time, and a good example of the heavy work necessary to keep us warm. The room had a brick floor and was the only room with a proper large wool carpet. Here, before the fire, was a hand-made wool mat, made with special rug wool in different colours that was wound round a wooden grooved ruler and cut to size - another job for me. It was then progged into a sack or hessian backing following a drawn pattern.

By the front door was the electric meter with, always, a small pile of shillings. You would be sitting comfortably reading your book when 'clunk' the last shilling would drop and everywhere would be plunged into darkness. Even I knew how to find a shilling, put it in the slot and turn the handle to restore the lights. I think most people in the town had electricity, but my farming Auntie still had neither gas nor electricity. They cooked with bottled gas, lit their rooms with oil or paraffin lamps and when my cousin and I went to bed we took a candle. The front door was not often opened as most callers came round the back. However this was where the milkman left his milk and rang to be paid. There were two sorts of milkman: one left pint bottles but the other had milk churns on a truck and, with a long handled measuring jug, poured the milk into a lidded enamel can that you left at the door as others did their 'empties'. My Leicester Auntie's milkman came with a horse drawn milk cart and I would hear him slowly clip-clopping past in the early morning. The horse learned the milk round and would know each house to stop at.

The sitting rooms would be warm and cosy but it was a different climate up in the bedrooms. My Auntie had the back bedroom and the rest of us the front. Bedrooms were for going to bed. There was no heating for other activities and even in summer no-one would think of taking a book upstairs to read. The only wireless was downstairs and of course there were no computers, television, play station etc. I did not play in the bedroom. All my toys, games and books were downstairs, and if a friend came to tea we would be in the back sitting room with the family.

The other main use was for being ill, and then sometimes a fire was lit. I had all the usual illnesses which then confined children to bed: measles, mumps, and chicken pox. Luckily I avoided scarlet fever, whooping cough and the much feared polio. My friend two doors away contracted polio the day before I was due to take him for his first day at school (I was six and he was five), and never walked again. My parents must have been very worried. There were no inoculations against these illnesses.

I liked to go to the bedrooms to look out of the windows. From the front window I could see the river and the big tree under which we played. I could see the railway crossing and the railway bridge over the river and watch as the gates opened and shut and see the trains chuffing slowly past. In fact in the bedroom I could hear the signalman the other side of the wall turning the wheel to open the gates and

When the signalman knew a train was coming he pulled the levers, which were attached to the points in the rails below by rods and wires, to control the direction of the train.

pulling the levers to change the points or the signals. I also saw him at dusk going out to light the gas lamp on the bridge. From Auntie's window I could see, beyond the gardens, the nearby ploughed fields and further away the grass fields with their high hawthorn hedges, where we children could go to pick daisies and buttercups and, skirting gingerly round the cows, explore the familiar yet foreign territory. (None of this is available to today's children as, in the 1970s, houses were built there as far as the eye can see.)

I could also see the signalman's pigsty right up against the fence. Once a year the pig killer came to kill the pig. A pig squeals with a high shrill note as its throat is cut and you hold your breath until it abruptly stops and then you know the pig is dead. Afterwards, instead of bringing a bucket of scraps for the pig he would cross back across the railway line with a bucket of blood.

Down the steep stairs from the living room was the 'cellar'. That's what we called it, although it was really a basement room with a fireplace, now boarded up, and a proper window. This was our kitchen, our bathroom and our wash house, the main drawback being that it had no water. There was no piped water or drainage in the house at all. The only tap was down the garden by the toilet. All drinking and cooking water was carried from there in buckets and waste water was either poured onto the garden or carried back to the drain by the tap. Mum, as the adult who did not go out to work, must have spent a lot of time down here. There were few short cuts to providing three meals a day for five people - no fish fingers or beefburgers for a quick meal. Neither was there a freezer to take out something ready-made, and indeed no fridge, so shopping had to be frequent. We had no gadgets like food processors or a microwave oven to make the work easier and quicker. However we no longer cooked on the coal range but with a proper gas cooker.

Dad, Auntie and I all came home for a cooked midday dinner, all at slightly different times, and then there was a high tea in the early evening. We were by no means well off, but with a housewife who knew how to cook, a garden full of fruit and vegetables, and chickens at the bottom of the garden I imagine we could be well fed. I know we always had a joint on Sunday (and I remember, like most people of my age, dried egg, which I particularly enjoyed as scrambled egg). There were always homemade cakes, pies and puddings, and although meat was not in generous supply we had it every day. Another of my jobs, aged 9+, was to queue at the pork butcher's on Saturdays for the weekend sausages, and a pork pie or a haslet.

The garden made a lot of difference to our diet as fruit and some vegetables were preserved for the winter and eggs were kept in isinglass liquid when the hens were laying well. Of course I didn't appreciate all this at the time. I was at school or off out to play, but I can see in retrospect how the household ran, as it continued to run like this through all my childhood. I don't recall helping at this time with cooking, making little cakes or special recipes for children. Perhaps time was always short. But I often helped with table setting and clearing and with washing-up. This wasn't for me an unwelcome chore. I remember always being happy to help with grown-up tasks. Well, usually!

I do remember helping with the washing, which again was hard work and took up much time. In the corner of the room was a large built-in copper with its own fire and chimney; but we didn't use that. No: we had a washing machine! It was square, stood on legs, and had a wringer with rollers on the top. The lid had paddles attached to the underside, and lifted up to pour in the hot water. On the lid was the handle that, when turned clockwise, anti-clockwise, on and on, moved the paddles to wash the clothes. I had a go at that and turned the handle of the wringer. The water was heated in a gas boiler and transferred to the washer by bucketfuls. This was all hard work, but not quite as basic as the dolly-tub method our neighbour used. This was a metal tub and the clothes were washed by moving the 'dolly', a piece of wooden equipment with arms to hold and legs to do the agitating, up and down turning as you did so. Every Monday Dad would fill the boiler with water from the underground rainwater cistern that was outside the back door. Sometimes the water was right at the top, but other times he threw a bucket on a string down to draw it up. Children had to stand well back when the cistern lid was open. Similarly water had to be drawn and heated for our baths. There was a large zinc bath for adults and a small one for me. The baby had an even smaller one of a sort of plastic, but had his bath by the fire upstairs. We had a small electric fire to give us some warmth. Needless to say no one bathed every night; we each took our turn once a week. The rest of the time we washed in a bowl at the zinc topped table where other water activities took place. At that time no house I visited had a bathroom, so there was nothing odd about these arrangements, except perhaps our lack of an indoor tap.

We had a long garden with a small lawn and flower beds and, beyond the toilet, the shed and the coal-shed, was the large vegetable garden and the chicken house and run. Dad spent most of his daylight hours when not at work out here, either working in the garden or making and mending in the shed. Many of our toys were homemade: a doll's house, a scooter (not a success as a wheel fell off the first time I ventured along the road), a wheelbarrow, a ride-on train. He also made small items of furniture often out of tea chests from the grocer's. In the same way as our clothes were homemade, so anything that could be made by an untaught man was made. If you needed a stool you made it, and if you needed a chicken house or rabbit hutch you made that too. His mother was widowed when he was five so he had many years of practice in DIY before becoming a father and householder.

I enjoyed the chickens, although when going in the run to scatter grain I was afraid of them pecking my legs. We fed them all sorts of scraps, and I liked going in with a bowl calling Chuuck! Chuck! and having them run when I threw the bits, well away from my legs. Best of all was collecting the eggs from the outside boxes and triumphantly taking them to the house still warm.

The toilet….well most people I knew had an outside toilet, but usually nearer the house than ours. After dark you went down there with a torch and inside switched on the larger lantern kept there. The short journey was dark and you had the usual illogical fear that something would jump out at you. The worst event however was a spider's web draping over my face. In winter of course you needed coat and shoes, and didn't linger, but in summer with the door open I used to pretend I was a gypsy sitting in my horse drawn caravan…or you could always read the toilet paper which was cut up newspaper threaded on a string.

I often had friends come to play in the garden. These were arrangements simply between me and the friends, Mum playing little part in my social life. We did all the usual things little girls do: tea parties with toys, making tents, games of families and school. But we also spent a lot of our time 'out to play' from about age seven, roaming about unaccompanied in the fields or along the lanes or the river on foot or on bikes. No one worried about us and we told no-one where we were going or had been, and if we did it was of interest to them rather than a cause for concern. Of course, on the occasions when there might have been, it seemed wiser not to mention it.

In 1950 my way of life changed again. Our family moved to a brand new spacious council house. At last a home fit for heroes. It had a large sunny kitchen where you could cook and eat and a through room for sitting and eating. There was a large square hall with space to hang coats, and a downstairs toilet, then three bedrooms and bathroom with toilet. At the back entrance was an indoor store, used to keep our new single-tub electric washing-machine and our bikes, and an indoor coal house. There was a garden front and back and, instead of a railway, a shop next door. There was no central heating of course; that was not expected in 1950. But what a change from what we had always known! I can remember Mum explaining how I should get up and go into the bathroom to wash, and how I was keen to get into the big bath with my little brother.

It was a few years before we had a television, and many before Mum felt she needed a fridge. We never had a freezer or an electric mixer or a phone or a car: these were not considered essentials.

The life I have described cannot be considered 'typical'. Then, as now, where and how you lived was determined partly by your income. Other Mums worked because they needed money, some because they had higher education. Few would have worked because they had too little to occupy them. Some Dads had cars. Some families owned their houses. Some children went to private schools. Some households had a daily help.

But this is life as I remember it.

Beyond the baby class

Mo Morgan

"When you finish your work, draw handwriting patterns on your boards." As the chalky dust specks glittered in the four wide beams of sunlight from the high windows of our new classroom, we thought that Miss Bell might have had to tell her baby starters of last year but not us. We were in the second class. We knew how to behave.

As we chanted our seven times table, the sing-song voices looked forward to playtime. We were allowed to practise our skipping for the exhibition, forty of us all working in time. Arms extended, you held the rope up high in front of you. With one toe pointed, standing on the very bottom of the loop, you gave your wrists a flicking twist and caught the ends securely by pressing with your thumb. We had a set programme of hopping, kicking, pointing, jumping steps which were counted in silence. If you made a mistake you got into the start position again and stood very still ready waiting for the stop, hop, step, step, start which was the signal for the next block to begin. What a fantastic feeling of working together!

We practised so much that everybody got it right at the demonstration. We were very proud of ourselves, but sat in absolute awe of another school who recited poetry all together in a great swell of sound that made you hold your breath as they charged on together in rhythm.

On Fridays, after school, came the journey to Nanna's house, where my Mum would be sitting in the kitchen by the range fire, laughing and chatting with her mother and sisters.

It was quite normal then for a six-year-old to be expected to negotiate the walk of a mile or so past all her friends' houses; to be trusted not to slip into the recreation ground for a turn on the swing, not to pick the flowers along the pathway edges, not to linger by the sweet-smelling jam-factory, not to peer into the windows of the printers trying to see what made the clacking noises, not to run across the road in front of a bicycle, not to be tempted to gaze into the library or the corner shop, not to stay listening to the blackbirds near the men's bowling club, but to race along, happy in the freedom and responsibility of finding the last tricky little bit of the journey, the way through to the short-cut to her grandmother's house amongst the trees.

A different world then, seen from now.

Student report

June Thexton

This is an edited extract from June's contribution to the 'Old Girls' Notes' of the County Grammar School for Girls in Barrow-in-Furness.

In 1950, I set out to continue my studies as a rather apprehensive 'fresher' at Leeds University. However, the feelings of apprehension and newness have little place in the life which rapidly engulfs you at this Yorkshire establishment of learning, where the introduction to the stern academic disciplines of one's subject and new vistas of thought occurs simultaneously with one's first experience of student life as a whole - of burning the midnight oil and the candle at both ends.

I went about my business, as have countless students before, among the tumble-down Department houses, which stand on cobbled streets, tree-shaded, still wearing an air of sleepy Victorian propriety. They are at the feet of the magnificent functional structures of concrete and steel which form the new University and are a far cry from those older institutes of learning, which are mentioned among us, if at all, only with reverence.

Rag Week, debates, Balls, folk dancing, play productions, beer drinking contests and yo-yo championships flourish unabashed by the academic progress achieved by the University proper, in the Union Building when lectures are over for the day (and sometimes when they aren't).

Having been an elected member of the Union's main Committee for three years I know, sometimes to my cost, that there are more serious sides to student life and that politics and religion gain a fair hearing. I know that there is much business done quietly and without fuss in regard to grants and students' welfare, vacation jobs, representation at international student affairs and in the orderly running of the Students' Building and all its many activities.

This year (1954), on what some call frivolously the lighter side, I have been Entertainments Secretary of the Union and have had a hectic time arranging Balls and Socials throughout the session.

My pièce de resistance was the Ball we held to celebrate the University's Jubilee on Charter Day in April which was attended by our Chancellor, the Princess Royal. After many headaches and sleepless nights all went well and nine hundred students sat down to dinner in the huge new refectory we had just acquired. Afterwards there was dancing to four bands and a cabaret put on for the Chancellor by the foreign students.

Also in connection with the Jubilee, I was lucky enough to be one of the eight students who were presented to the Queen Mother and entertained her to tea when she came to be patron to our celebrations and accept an honorary degree. This was certainly a wonderful experience and one which I shall always remember as the Queen Mother seemed so genuinely interested in all she saw and in the people she met.

Leeds is a somewhat workaday university with its large number of technological students, its connection with the local wool trade and the aura of Yorkshire joviality and business sense which surrounds it.

But I have been lucky in witnessing two very impressive ceremonies which have endowed it with pageantry and traditional dignity. At the installation of the Princess Royal as our Chancellor in 1951 and again this year at the Jubilee of the university's foundation, I have seen the assembly of the academic staff and senate, representatives from universities all over the world, local dignitaries, High Court judges and the impressive sword of the

County of York carried in the traditional fashion process through the crowded, silent Town Hall. They formed a scene of splendour which was overawing to a mere undergraduate like myself. I 'heard all, saw all and said nowt', but the wealth of colour of the glorious robes of the company, especially the Queen Mother and the Princess Royal, and the clear fanfare of the trumpeters and singing of the choir would have been sufficient to make the most voluble person speechless.

It gave us all a great thrill and an unexpected feeling of pride to think that the old traditions were being maintained at out relatively new university.

Now that my four years are over, I realize that I may have spent too much time indulging in student affairs, both serious and hilarious, even if I didn't get round to the beer drinking competition.

Barrow-in-Furness County Grammar School for Girls

OLD GIRLS' NOTES

- - - -

OFFICERS, 1955

President : The Headmistress of the School, Miss J. W. Wells, M.A. (Oxon).
Vice-Presidents : Mrs. S. I. Childs, Miss M. J. Hillier, Miss M. Pratt.
Secretary : Mrs. Pettingale (Mary Kendall), 54, Highlands Avenue.
Assistant Secretary : Muriel Todd, 31, John Street.
Treasurer : Jeanne Kilburn, 41, Dartmouth Street.
Magazine Correspondent : Joan Cathcart, 100, Ocean Road.
Committee : Staff Member : Miss W. M. Ford.
Vickerstown : Mrs. Whittall (Joan Bazley), 116, Hartington Street.
South Walney : Vera Brull, 22, Liverpool Street.
Barrow Island : Delia Pinington, 82, Island Road.
Roose : Enid Jackson, 103, Poplar Grove.
Salthouse : Betty Yarr, 200, Marsh Street.
Central : Jean Tollitt, 28, Coulton Street.
Hindpool : Audrey Cameron, 10, Farm Street.
Ainslie Street : Yvonne Thorp, 27, Middle Hill.
White House : Jessie Haslam, 6, West Avenue.
Fairfield Lane : Mrs. Chadderton (Rozel Williams), 30, Fairfield Lane.
Furness Park Road : Mrs. Burns (Doris Hall), 23, Lord Street.
Hawcoat : Mrs. Webber (Freda Thompson), 5, Baldwin Street.
Beacon Hill : Margaret Kemp, 3, Highlands Avenue.
Auditors : Jean Cleland, Mrs. Kinnish (Doris Giles).

- - - -

FROM THE PRESIDENT

The time and opportunity has again returned for me to send my greetings to all members of the Old Girls' Club through the medium of the magazine. The last twelve months have brought changes to school, some of which, I know, many will read with regret

1951

	Unrest in Middle East (assassinations in Iran, Jordan, Syria, Pakistan)
	Closer European integration (iron and steel)
	NHS reforms
	Cooling relations with USSR leading to the 'Cold War'
	School Leaving Certificates were replaced by GCE 'O' and 'A' Levels
	The first residential tower block was constructed, in Harlow New Town
	First Guidebook in Pevsner's *Buildings of Britian* series
	First edition of Postgate's *The Good Food Guide*
	Turn indicators on cars introduced – most still used hand signals
January	**Board of Film Censors introduced X ratings**
March	Dennis the Menace appeared in the *Beano* comic
	UNIVAC in the USA launched the first widely used commercial computer
April	The Stone of Scone found in Forfar
	Battle of the Imjin River in the Korean War won by China
	Prescription charges announced for dental care and spectacles, to help with the costs of the Korean War
May	**The Festival of Britain opened on London's South Bank: Royal Festival Hall, Dome of Discovery, Skylon (ended on September 30)**

	First broadcast of *The Goon Show* on radio
	Easington Colliery explosion killed 83 miners
	'Peaceful liberation' of Tibet by China; Dalai Lama decided to go to India
	First thermonuclear boosted atomic bomb tested by US
June	Burgess and Maclean (spies) defected to USSR
July	*Show Boat* was projected in Technicolor from Empire State Building, NY
August	First Miss World beauty pageant, held at the Festival of Britain
September	Forest fires over Europe caused 'blue sun'
	Britain boycotted Iran after it nationalised its oilfields
October	Churchill became Prime Minister again
	Zebra pedestrian crossings introduced
November	More troops sent to Suez Canal zone, and families are evacuated
	Lyons Corner Houses (restaurants) devised and used LEO, a room-sized 6000 valve computer, to operate its accounts and logistics
December	**State of emergency in Egypt; riots**

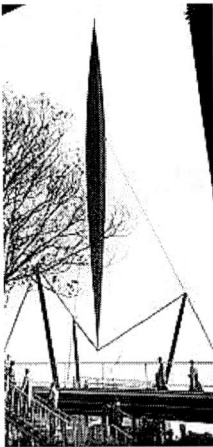

1951: Left: the Skylon Tower at the Festival of Britain on London's South Bank.

Below: the view from across the River Thames of part of the site including the Dome of Discovery.

Festival, Co-op string and births

Audrey Stacey

In 1951 we went to the Festival of Britain on London's South Bank several times. What I remember most about it was the Skylon on the South Bank and the Guinness clock at Battersea Festival Gardens. The clock was tall and had a figure of a toucan which was behind doors below the clock face. Every quarter of an hour the toucan and other figures came out and did a turn. The toucan, with its bright orange beak, was used a lot in advertising Guinness on posters. When the Festival was over the clock was displayed on tour around Britain.

The fun fair at the Battersea Festival Gardens also had a hall of mirrors which distorted your face and body into different shapes. There was an upside-down house, which you went into and it whizzed you round and round turning you upside down, so you came out feeling giddy. We went into it several times, being gluttons for punishment.

Audrey's children and friend sitting below the Guinness clock in 1955: the clock doors are open but the toucan is hidden by a bush in this photo.

The Skylon on the South

117

Bank site was a very tall (300 feet high) pencil-like structure, pointed at both ends and held up by wires. It was suspended in the air, the lower point being 50 feet from the ground. It seemed amazing that it never blew over.

From the 1950s I also have sharp memories of going to the Co-op grocery, and can still picture the shop. The counter was L-shaped. We went to the part of the counter on the left for bacon, ham, cheese and other dairy products. They used to cut the butter from a large block and pat the portions with wooden paddles into a neat shape. Cheese was cut with a wire. The assistant (nearly always male) took your purchases round to a shelf behind the other part of the counter where you chose your sugar, sauces, tins etc. Sugar was weighed into a blue paper bag. Biscuits were displayed in a line of glass-covered tins, so that you could make a choice. Broken biscuits were much cheaper.

You paid your money and it was put in a metal cup which the assistant twisted onto an overhead fitting. He pulled a lever and the cup went along a wire to a corner where the cashier sat. He sent the change back, plus the tokens (or 'cheques') for the dividend. The assistant made your groceries into a neat parcel, no matter what shape they were, tins and all, and wrapped it in brown paper and tied it criss-cross with string. He wound the string round his hand and snapped it without scissors. I've often thought about that and wondered how it worked.

Our daughter was born in 1952 and our son in 1953. They were born in a nursing home in Bristol. I went to my GP for ante-natal checks, and if he wanted a sample of urine he would say 'Pop behind the screen and there is a little piddle pot to use'. When I finally went to the ante-natal clinic, I found Mortimer House and walked in through the front door and was greeted by the Matron, who demanded sharply "What are you doing here?" When I told her she directed me crossly to go outside and round the corner to another door. Matrons ruled the roost in those days.

The morning when I realised that the baby was on its way, the chimney sweep turned up. When he finished I cleaned the floor after him while the labour pains were continuing. I finally made my way to the nursing home (we had no telephone to call for help), and was on my own as my husband was at work. I was shown into a bed. Husbands were not allowed to be present at the birth in those days. Jane was finally born the following morning. She was a healthy 8-pounder, but, as with all babies, she was taken away to the nursery and was only brought back to me at the prescribed feeding times. Fathers were permitted to look at their baby through a glass window. On this occasion a kindly nurse allowed Bob to hold Jane in his arms. He was taken aback and thrilled by the excitement.

Like all new mothers I was not allowed to set foot out of the bed for ten days (14 days if you had had to have stitches). You crawled to the end of the bed, at bed-making times, and crawled back up again when the nurses had finished.

Visiting times were very strict. When my father came to see his granddaughter he was not allowed into the building. As

New baby Simon, with Jane.

my bed was near the window, though, I could wave to him as he stood on the road. The same happened when our son, Simon, was born, but this time there was no kindly nurse to allow Bob to hold him.

How times have changed! Nowadays mothers can be seen out shopping a couple of days after the birth.

Shades of the Festival

Lesley Wheeler

The Festival of Britain in 1951, when I was three-years-old, is a vague childhood memory for me. I know we went up to Battersea Pleasure Gardens and the Fun Fair on the tube from Harrow-on-the-Hill, and my father has told me it was the last time for 30 years that we saw my Uncle Rich, his younger brother, before he emigrated to New Zealand.

The story behind that decision included the sudden and traumatic death of their parents when Rich was only 13, the struggle to keep the children and home together by the two elder sisters and the forlorn efforts of a 'housekeeper' assigned by Social Services and deeply resented by Rich. In the aftermath of the Depression in the Medway towns he was given a roof over his head by the sister who got married at 22, giving up her aspirations to be a teacher in order to 'keep house'. A few years later he had been excited and carried along by the public fervour at the outbreak of war and immediately signed up for the Army. Within four months he had been trained, drilled, kitted out, sent overseas to battle and captured in Cyprus. He spent the next five years in a Prisoner of War Camp in Italy, together with many ANZAC troops that he got friendly with. He never talked about those years, but met a girl on the boat passage whom he later married and had a family, work and a settled life in Wellington and Wanganui. His letters talk of getting his Christmas Red Cross parcel in March, with its pyjamas (kept for special Sunday 'leisure-wear'), matches and stationery. I recall Rich coming to our house and

120

standing in the dark passageway, looking like a young version of my Dad.

At the Battersea Fun Fair I remember trailing about in huge crowds, realising that I might get lost, sitting on my Dad's shoulders in the night air and some fantastic fireworks, culminating in one that had a crown and words written in fire. The fantastic celebration of British design, architecture and modern art in the Dome and Pavilions on the South Bank site in 1951 meant nothing to me. The planning for four post-war years to include many big exhibits travelling round Britain was beyond my understanding. The innovations of architecture and urban planning did not affect Harrow shops and schools for many years, and I was oblivious to the significance of the Great Exhibition at Crystal Palace a century before. On the other hand, the words Big Dipper came into my consciousness. Morale-boosting events, shows and celebrations became more common again. Public confidence and cultural awakening grew after years of rationing and austerity. The South Bank became a byword for music, experimental events and culture for me in my teenage years. I was influenced indirectly by the impact on my parents, schooling, artistic licence, new buildings and the social awareness of art in the environment.

1951: across the Atlantic, too, technology was advancing with the launching of UNIVAC's first commercial computer, with what now seems to be a very large console and tape spools.

The Festival of Britain promising, as it did, to complement the new security and health of the fledgling Welfare State, had little impression on me at the time, but I suspect it made a huge difference to my life and my generation in ways that can only be surmised.

Dancing days

Joan Congleton

The 1950s were a time of optimism in Britain, with politicians promising a better future and families trying to heal the emotional scars of the war. For my tap-dancing class display at the Oxford Galleries the teacher had managed to obtain a job lot of blackout material left over from the war, and a never ending roll of red, white and blue ribbon from the victory celebrations with which to turn out short full-skirted black frocks made by mothers or local dressmakers. With loud metallic sounds resounding on the wooden floor from our brilliant tap shoes thirty girls danced as if there was no tomorrow. After dark days of war that brilliant evening symbolised our hopes for prosperity and happiness. In 1950, although clothes rationing continued, Dior's New Look dominated the fashion world, and it was wonderful for ordinary women to discard their turbans and wrap-around pinafores and think of dressing fashionably again.

Mrs Dodson, our local dressmaker, was a wizard on her Singer sewing machine and with bright brown eyes, gold-rimmed spectacles and long thin hands she conjured up 'that look' for me. Mum had managed to buy enough grey flannel from Farnon's in Nun Street to make a suit with a full skirt almost to the ankles, a tight-fitting jacket which flounced below the waist, a white rayon blouse and a bright red artist's bow to complete the image. My friends, who wore similar outfits, and I thought we were the bees-knees as we paraded into Fenwick's tea-room to the sound of Willie Walker and his band.

122

The West End Congregational Church was the only one in my locality to have a Saturday night dance, and was known as the 'West End Conga'. One of the girls there had an uncle who was a professional dancer and, to the sound of a gramophone, he kindly and patiently taught the correct steps and rhythms for the quick-step, slow foxtrot, tango and many more (no discos then). My favourite was the moonlight saunter, and I was the envy of all the girls as I glided across the floor wearing nylon stockings, a new fashion item from America which were in my possession – I know not how.

A Singer sewing machine from the 1950s, operated by a foot treadle.

The 1944 Education Act had given those who were suited to an academic education the opportunity for higher education, but in fact in 1951 I was one of only four girls who entered the sixth form at Rutherford High School. Many others, together with their parents, considered the professions 'were not for the likes of us'; consequently there were psychological barriers to be overcome.

My friend Margaret and I needed to find paid employment during the school holidays. When mid-December came she and I would set off in the dark and cold to catch a bus to start work at 7am at the Post Office in Orchard Street near the Central Station. Our head-teacher, Miss Wood, frowned upon us when we asked her permission to do temporary work, and only agreed reluctantly when we said we would have to leave school if we didn't earn some money.

So, along with adult women, we stood from early morning till 3pm, with a half-hour break for lunch, facing envelopes the right way up and placing them on a conveyor belt at eye level ready for sorting in another area. There was a trough below the belt and, just as we emptied it, the regular postmen came with sacks brimming with more envelopes and tipped them into the trough for facing. It was never ending.

To relieve the boredom one day Margaret and I began to sing the carols due to be sung at the school's carol service, an event we were sadly to miss. Everyone seemed to enjoy this and each day would request their favourites, while the supervisor postman gave us the first opportunity to work overtime.

The following Christmas we were promoted to the sorting department. Here again the methods were manual, though we had the luxury of sitting on a solid polished wooden stool with an axle which allowed us to swing from side to side to reach the pigeon holes in front of us. These were each named with the counties and districts of the UK, with one marked 'Abroad'.

A poignant memory of 1952 is of the bitterly cold February morning when our headmistress, Miss Wood, announced the death of King George VI to a group of sixth-formers. We stood in the dark school corridor with blank faces as we didn't know how to react, and Miss Wood was rather cross. As the news sank in all over the country there was great sadness, but this changed to feelings of tenderness and hope as the young Queen stepped down from the aeroplane that flew her and her husband back home from Africa. 'The King is dead: long live the Queen' has become a reality in this year of her Diamond Jubilee.

For me the years 1953-5 were spent at Darlington Teacher Training College. I was one of only a few girls from a working class background there, but I felt privileged, loved the course and worked hard. The college was ahead of its time, introducing new active methods of learning and group work, frowning on too much formal work with children sitting in rows. It is a pity the training colleges were abolished as they did an excellent specialised job. We had a tutor for every subject we were to teach and whom we observed working in the classroom with children.

A typical dress style for dancing in the 1950s.

There was play for the students, too, especially at the Saturday dances where only army officers from the nearby Catterick camp could attend. In readiness for the evening ahead we girls in the dormitories put our hair in curlers, and swapped clothes and make-up. Again the music was from records on a gramophone with one student put in charge.

At the end of the academic year there was a live band at the 'Formal' when we could have an invited guest. For these I wore a lemon organdie dress, sprigged with white flowers. This was a bridesmaid dress, complete with a bolero which I removed as the temperature in the hall rose with the exertions of *Strip the Willow* and *Gay Gordons*, when a Scottish soldier stood on one of the cupboards to play his bagpipes. During the interval the tutor on duty would wheel in a trolley laden with glasses of orange juice. At 11pm it was time for the men to leave the premises and then the main door was locked with great ceremony.

At the time of the Festival of Britain in 1951, Mum and Dad had joined the people from all parts of the UK who went to London to see the fairground attractions but mainly to marvel at the exhibition demonstrating how design, science and technology were to take Britain into a brave new world.

The Festival brochure, price 2s 6d (12½p).

For a much deserved treat they had gone on their own leaving me in charge at home. On their return laden with Festival souvenirs, their faces reflected the fun and inspiring experiences they had had and hope for the years of growth that there were to be ahead.

My first "dress-up" do

Mary Dodds

My school arranged for us to have pen pals in Paris and I wrote regularly to Françoise in English and she answered in French. In 1951 my class took a trip to Paris to visit our pen pals. I remember having to travel in school uniform which wasn't very 'cool'. I spent a lovely day with Françoise, her mother and brother. The meal her mother provided lasted three hours. There was course after course with grapes and fruit in between. We could hardly move but it was a good day. Trips were planned to Nôtre Dame, Sacré Coeur, Arc de Triomphe and Napoleon's Tomb and of course a trip up the Eiffel Tower. The highlight for me was the visit to the Louvre and seeing the Mona Lisa.

During the fifties I was a member of the Church Choir and two Youth Clubs and enjoyed playing table tennis, netball, doing handicrafts and dancing. I was also studying for my Commercial exams. It was during my time at the Youth Club that a group of us went to a Youth Hostel at Thropton. One morning we went for a walk and spent most of the time killing rabbits to put them out of their misery because they were suffering from myxomatosis.

After I left school I started work immediately in an office and had the good fortune to have a super boss who trained me in all aspects of office procedures. In my spare time I joined a Community Centre which had a good programme for young people. Here I decided to investigate the possibility of becoming a youth worker, something which I achieved in later years.

In the same year, we had a youth club member who came to the Friday night 'hop' in a full *Teddy Boy* outfit. It did cause a stir, with his DA (duck's arse) haircut, long blue jacket and drainpipe trousers at the end of which were blue suede shoes. He caused such a stir that the music stopped and we all stood and stared, some of the boys jeering and calling him names.

Teddy Boy suede shoes were known as 'brothel creepers'.

In 1955 I went to my first 'dress up' do at the Banqueting Hall in Jesmond. I nearly didn't get there as my friend had a partner and I hadn't. She told me not to worry as she would find someone for me. I had no need to worry indeed as the person she picked for me was a wonderful dancer, and after he and I danced our first dance it was 'heaven'. Then half-way through the evening my friend told me that my partner was a dance instructor at the Newbiggin Dance Studios. I got very nervous at that point but he put me at my ease and we had a lovely evening. I often wonder what happened to him.

I met my husband-to-be who was a soldier on leave from Germany. We were married in September 1958 and I was invited to spend Christmas in Germany with my husband and stay with his friends. The only set-back was that I worked for the Co-operative Wholesale Society and when I asked for leave my boss wasn't very pleased. They didn't encourage married women to work for them as they were worried that women would become pregnant and have to leave. As they would not give me leave to go to Germany I had to leave my work. I was newly married and looking forward to spending time with my husband.

I flew from Woolsington (now Newcastle) Airport, which consisted of wooden huts at that time. We walked across the tarmac to board the plane. The flight was bumpy and very cold.

It was strange hearing the German language for the first time and when one of the children of the family I stayed with changed from English to German in mid-sentence it made me feel very inadequate.

1952

	Polio epidemic
	First TV detector vans
February	**King George VI died of lung cancer and was succeeded by Queen Elizabeth II**
	First TV detector vans in operation
	Wartime ID cards abandoned
April	First post-war university established, Southampton
May	**De Havilland Comet was the world's first jet airliner, with maiden flight from London to Johannesburg**
	First woman to sail the Atlantic single-handed, Ann Davison
June	NHS prescription charge of 1/- (5p) imposed
	Reindeer reintroduced to Scotland
	The *Diary of Ann Frank* published
August	Flood at Lynmouth, Devon, killed 34 people
September	Farnborough Airshow crash killed 31 people
	Charlie Chaplin refused entry to the USA for supposed communist tendency
	200th anniversary of the change from the Julian to the Gregorian calendar, when Wednesday Sept 2 was followed by Thursday Sept 14
October	**Tea rationing ended after 13 years**
	UK exploded its first atomic bomb, Monte Bello Islands, Australia
	Rail crash in North London killed 108 people
	Welsh republican group tried to blow up a pipe taking water to Birmingham

	Mau Mau uprising in Kenya, biological warfare used to kill cattle
November	First performance of Christie's *The Mousetrap*
	Scottish protests at a GPO pillar box inscribed with Elizabeth **II**
	US detonated first hydrogen bomb, Marshall Islands
December	**A 6-day Great Smog in London caused traffic chaos and about 4000 deaths**
	End of Utility Furniture scheme
	BBC TV's first showing of *The Flowerpot Men*

1952: the world's first jet liner, the De Havilland Comet.

Not a touchy-feely era

Lydia Koelmans

I was born in 1948, so the 1950s were the decade of my childhood. As such, I was a 'post-war bulge baby': a term I hated as a child, because I thought it made me sound fat or misshapen. As I was her firstborn, my mother was determined to do things right and follow the rules of the then childcare guru, Dr Spock, which meant I was left crying, alone, until it was time for my next four-hourly feed. A night-time feed, even for a newborn, was quite out of the question. This was the recommended way of ensuring a child did not grow up spoilt. As was considered normal, I was toilet trained at 12 months. Babies were not considered to need toys and there was neither the quantity nor the quality of colourful toys there is today. It was enough to have a rattle, a soft toy, wooden blocks often made by dads, and we had empty cotton reels on a string for a train. At my first birthday, my father recorded that my favourite toy was 'a jam jar and a rubber band'. I was put in a pink wooden playpen and probably chewed the lead-painted bars.

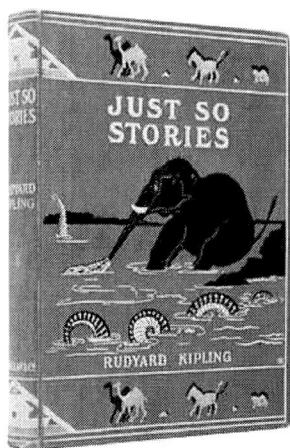

Rudyard Kipling's Just So Stories; the cover illustrates how the elephant got his trunk.

Our parents used to read to us 'Winnie the Pooh' and the 'Just So Stories'. During my childhood, I enjoyed climbing trees, fishing for minnows and tadpoles, searching for fossils and exploring rock pools, learning to recognise all the wild flowers, sailing boats on the pond,

131

picnics, swings and slides in the park, colouring books and playing with the scraps of fabric in my mother's ragbag and her large store of buttons (kept in a National Dried Milk tin). My father made me a doll's house and bagatelle board. We had seaside holidays and unsophisticated birthday parties at home with games like Pass the Parcel and Pin the Tail on the Donkey. Our family played paper-and-pencil games (hangman, noughts and crosses, quizzes), many different card games, and simple board games (Snakes and Ladders, Ludo). I also enjoyed hand-embroidering tray cloths for my trousseau/bottom drawer. And I had climbed many of the highest mountains in England by the time I was ten.

My father's values were working-class, Methodist, teetotal, pacifist and he voted Labour; my mother was middle-class. Although both my parents became teachers, at the start of the decade we had neither fridge, nor TV, nor car. Our family never did acquire an automatic washing machine or central heating. White cottons and linens (collars, blouses, serviettes, sheets etc) had to be starched before they were ironed. The radio was called a wireless. Our bedrooms were unheated, and in winter we awoke to wonderful frost patterns on the inside of the windows, sometimes so thick that the net curtains were embedded into the ice. When eventually we borrowed a car for a holiday in the Lake District, it had to be cranked up by a starting handle. The handbrake didn't work, so we carried around chocks to put behind the wheels, in case the car stopped on a hill and had to be pushed. Legally on the road there were cars that had extensive gaping and rusting holes in the bodywork or even car floor.

Richard and Lydia standing on an immaculately scrubbed doorstep with the edges whitened.

132

Our first TV was black and white and initially had only one channel, BBC. One programme shown, *The Black and White Minstrel Show*, was in highly dubious taste, featuring rows of men, half of whom were grotesquely blacked up and with whitened lips, strutting and singing.

Bed changing was a weekly Saturday morning ritual, called 'top to bottoming'. There were no duvets, fitted sheets or polycotton, and, in the 1950s, not even as yet Brentford Nylon's *Bri-nylon*. We had white, cotton, flat sheets bearing the utility mark, and which had to be ironed - plus blankets and eiderdowns. The idea was that the lower sheet got washed each week, and the previous top sheet became the new bottom sheet, secured round the mattress with 'hospital corners'. When any of the sheets got very thin in the middle, they would be 'sides-to-middled,' which entailed cutting them in two lengthways, and sewing the pieces together with the worn bits at the edges.. When sheets became too far gone even for this, good parts were salvaged to make pillow cases and cot sheets. I grew up with recycling. We had a salvage sack into which we put all used newspaper, and old woollens were sent off to make *shoddy*. By the age of nine, I was darning all my father's socks. Daddy used to pick up in the street things that might come in useful such as bits of string and nails, and he ended up making holes in his pockets, so my mother had a stock of replacement pockets to sew onto his trousers. A rag-and-bone man used to come round on a horse and cart to take away unwanted goods or scrap.

We always sat round a table for meals, and we had to ask to leave the table when we had finished. We were allowed to ask for one sweet, but only at the end of a meal. Pubs were places for men only and our family never ate out in restaurants in the 1950s. I remember when I had a bad cold my mother preparing a 'poultice'; this was a smelly, yellow, heavy, warm, moist, large mass of stuff that was plastered onto a cloth and strapped around the front of my chest. I have no idea what it contained.

We used to write lots of long letters by hand, and the post was collected from the pillar box even on Sundays. There was one rate, and two next-day deliveries: early morning and early afternoon. Phone calls were connected by a human operator, and to use public call boxes you had to press button A or button B.

A hot iron and MEND-A-TEAR make the neatest, quickest, cleanest repair.

JOHN BULL MEND-A-TEAR

G4
Mend-a-Tear

MENDS WITHOUT STITCHES

Mend-a Tear's contribution to make-do-and-mend.

Toilet paper was hard, scratchy and totally non-absorbent (Izal) and in some places consisted of pieces of hand-torn newspaper secured on a string. As our feet grew, we had them measured and shoes fitted every time using the latest technology: X-rays showing the foot bones inside the shoes. By the early 60s, I was getting my shoes re-heeled (several times each pair), and my hair cut, each for 6d (2½p). I sometimes used to sleep with horrendously uncomfortable metal rollers in my hair all night, to curl it.

Walking the 1½ miles each way, mainly over fields, I started school at the age of five in a class of 48, never having been to nursery school, playgroup or the like, and in the first year I caught measles, chicken pox, mumps and more. I was taught to read with *Janet and John* books. Playtime was an intimidating affair involving large raucous gangs striding about arm-over-arm chanting: "Anyone-want-to-play-cowboys-and-Indians-no-girls-allowed." Another game involved correctly guessing the names of film stars from their initials and I became very good at this, albeit without even knowing what a film star was. Other yard games were hopscotch, jacks, and group or individual skipping games. I developed two separate ways of speaking: received BBC English at home, and short 'a's at school, for self-preservation in both settings. School

134

toilets were in a cold and smelly outside block and I used to avoid drinking so as not to need them. We chanted our times tables, and had daily spelling tests. There was no talking in class, and if anyone misbehaved they got corporal punishment (which could involve shaking, rapping on the knuckles with a ruler – or the cane, I think). One teacher used to throw the chalk at pupils, hard. I remember being smacked by my father at home, towards the end of the 1950s (for lying that I had cleaned my teeth when my toothbrush was dry).

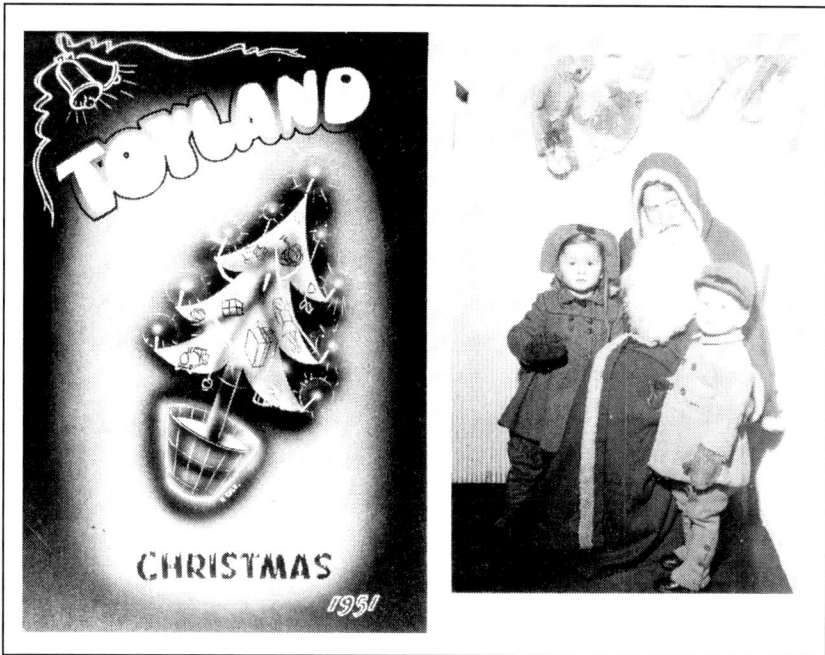

A postcard of Lydia and brother Richard sent to their grandparents, 1951.

At primary school I used to write with a pen, composed of a wooden holder and a replaceable nib that you dipped into an inkwell that was part of the school desk. Teachers would come round to fill the inkwells from a huge bottle of ink. At secondary school we used fountain pens containing a rubber bladder that you filled by suction by dipping the pen into ink and depressing and releasing a lever.

Towards the end of the decade, once a week we would be frogmarched from school to the local swimming baths and forced into the smelly chlorinated water (the best way to overcome fears, we were told). We were yelled at all the time to hurry while we tugged our clothes back onto scarcely dry bodies before downing a scalding cup of watery cocoa and being rushed (still in crocodile formation) back to school, stitch in our sides, in time for the next lesson. No showers, and our costumes had to be wrung out in a mangle. I wore a regulation black costume and a white rubber swimming cap.

In the winter I wore a woollen vest, and also throughout my childhood a *liberty bodice*. This was a misnomer as far as I was concerned because it seemed to be a tight, restrictive padded undergarment that you wore on top of the vest for extra warmth, and which fastened with seemingly millions of tiny rubber buttons. My twelfth birthday present from my mother was my first nylon stockings (these had to be darned, with thread called 'Make Do and Mend,' if you snagged them) and a suspender belt. It was followed shortly after by a whalebone corset (not real whalebone but it did have 'bones' that stuck into you, although I wasn't even fat), and I got the impression that the body was a thing to be hidden, disguised, strapped in and flattened. My mother sewed and knitted clothes for me: skirts with crossover straps to keep them up and a multicoloured jumper that I loved. Despite being the firstborn, I still wore a lot of 'hand me down' clothes, including already superseded uniform styles. Mainstay uniform at secondary school, where I started at the end of the decade, was the 'gymslip', an unbecoming garment that was not worn for gym. We had to wear voluminous, thick, regulation navy blue knickers. These were not hand-me-downs, because I remember being taken by my mother to the uniform shop, where she announced loud enough for the whole shop to hear, 'She takes the biggest size' (this was not true but ensured said knickers were even more voluminous than they needed to be). Likewise the regulation coat, a navy 'gabardine', was bought so big that it had first to be turned up, and the very same coat was still dropping off my shoulders by the Upper Sixth. Moreover it had to double as my weekend coat, too, until anoraks came in. Boys wore long socks held up by elastic garters and my brother wore short trousers throughout primary school. Men wore suits, and used to doff their cap or bowler hat to people in the

Lydia's embroidery sampler (the original is in bright colours).

street. As a child I was taught to call any man I didn't know, a 'gentleman'. On Sundays we went to the local Anglican Church, which was formal, cold and dark. I was taught by my mother that you must always wear a hat in church, and even in summer I had to put on little white cotton gloves for church (church uniform?). Trousers were generally considered unfeminine on women.

It was received knowledge that unless they found a husband at least before the end of their twenties, women were 'on the shelf' – but you were not allowed to show any interest in the opposite sex, for fear of being thought 'forward'. Sex was not talked about and you grew up knowing next to nothing about it. There was not a lot of openness: doctors sometimes thought it best not to tell their patients the worst, even when they asked, and childhood bereavements were often 'swept under the carpet'. On finding her birth certificate as a young adult, my cousin discovered a 'skeleton in the cupboard,' as it showed that the person she had grown up to think of as her mother was, in fact, her step-mother.

People with disabilities were not in much evidence in public, and there were certainly no measures to help them compete on an equal footing. My father used to get job interviews easily, but then had great difficulty in actually getting any work, in spite of his first class degree from Oxford, because he had a visible difficulty which caused employers to come up with spurious excuses not to take him on. My brother was taught from a young age that crying was 'unmanly'; meanwhile if we girls were distressed we would be either distracted or shamed out of it. The only people to hold hands in the street were parents with their young children. The 1950s were most definitely not a touchy-feely era.

Long days for a young chemist

Alec Bamford

I left school at 16, wishing to have a job in a chemistry laboratory. There was a number of firms in Leicester, about ten miles from my village, that had laboratories and employed 'lab boys' and 'lab girls', but there were no places available at first. Finally at the end of September I had a job in the Wolsey research laboratory. Wolsey had four establishments in Leicester: offices, two knitwear factories and a dyeing and finishing works on the bank of the canal. The work of the laboratory was mainly concerned with finding the best method to lessen shrinking of the knitted woollen underwear and socks. My weekly wage was thirty shillings (£1/10/- or £1.50 in today's money). After a year I had a huge rise to 50/- (£2.50) a week.

The research laboratory was on the second floor of one of the knitwear factories. From the second floor landing a door led into the lab. In front was the door to the office, to the right a corridor, next to the office the balance room and small library, then an open plan area. An open path was ahead with three double benches to the left at right angles to it. There were four graduate chemists and five boys. We were allowed two half-days a week to attend 'the Tech' - the Leicester College of Art and Technology. We were also expected to attend there regularly for three hours on two or three evenings (depending on the subjects studied and level) and every Saturday morning during term times. By the office door, set vertically, was a time-clock. We turned a rotor arm to our number and pushed its horizontal end into the hole below to ring a bell as it recorded our arrival, hoping it was still before 8am, our start time. The day went on till 6pm, except that we were allowed to leave at 5p.m on Tech nights.

To be at work on time, I had to be down the road for the 7.15am bus, which took about 30 minutes to Leicester. Then came a gallop across the centre of the city and on to a city bus, which fortunately turned into the road I wanted with a stop almost opposite the factory. There was a morning break in the Works canteen (the graduates used the Staff canteen) to which people took their own mug (for the lab boys a glass beaker). We then had a cooked lunch and an afternoon break with our own sandwiches on Tech nights. We sat with several of the foremen. After the Tech classes ended at 9pm on the second floor of the college, I had to race down the flights of stairs to the ground floor and janitor's little office and down 15 more steps to the main door followed by another 15 to pavement level. Then it was down the road, over the canal bridge, turn left and reach my bus stop about halfway down the first section of Western Boulevard for the 9.15 departure, arriving home about a quarter to ten - and then being up and ready for the 7.15 bus next morning.

In December of the following year, we learned that the higher powers had decided to close the lab next March, so I was made redundant before I was 18. As a first step, I was moved to the Dyeing and Finishing Works in January: It was further along the road from the factory and a 5+ minute walk along the canal bank. Time-keeping was more relaxed here: there was very little for me to do there except my Tech homework and through January I spent a lot of time close to the radiator to try to keep warm in this barn of a lab. In a corner of the lab was a great heap of parcels. Occasionally the other, older, lab boy would open one of these packets to see what had been returned. Mostly they were ladies' vests with the covering letter saying that they had shrunk in the first wash. Several sinkfuls of warm water washed out what seemed like enough soap for a week's wash and the vest would be restored to size and fluffiness and so earn the standard reply - 'please rinse more thoroughly'.

Carols amongst the barrels in 1952 at the BB Chemical Co: Alec is at the extreme left.

In March 1952 I had a new job, in one of the dozen laboratories of BB Chemical Co Ltd. The name of the firm came from the parent company, the US Boston Blacking Chemical Co. They opened up a factory in England in the shoe-making area of Leicestershire-Northamptonshire. and their subtitle was 'Manufacturers of shoe finishers and adhesives'. The company now calls itself *Bostik*. There were about the same number of male and female lab assistants and the Shoe Finishing Laboratory was in the charge of twin sisters. Start time was 8.30 here, but we had to put in a proper day's work. Morning break and midday meal were in the Staff canteen and afternoon tea break in the lab round the big table where we wrote our reports and used the mechanical, turn-the-handle calculator. Here we had a Works Outing, and of course in 1953 it was a train trip to London on the Saturday of Coronation Week. I don't remember the outings continuing after that.

140

1953

	Linear B, a Minoan language revealed to be Ancient Greek by Ventris
	First espresso bar opened in London
	G-Plan furniture introduced
January	Car ferry from Scotland to N Ireland sank with loss of 133 people
	North Sea flood on East Anglian coast killed hundreds
February	**Sweet rationing ended**
March	Queen Mary, the grandmother of Queen Elizabeth II, died of lung cancer
	Stalin died
	The murders at 10 Rillington Place were uncovered (8 bodies)
April	The first James Bond novel by Ian Fleming was published, *Casino Royale*
	Watson and Crick announced the discovery of DNA in the journal *Nature*
May	First FA Cup Final to be televised (Blackpool win over Bolton)
	Edmund Hillary and Tenzing Norgay reached the top of Mount Everest
June	Highest ever rainfall (80mm in 30 minutes), Eskdalemuir in the Scottish Borders
	Coronation of Queen Elizabeth II
July	First European Economic Community Assembly met in Strasbourg
August	**England cricket team defeated Australia to win the Ashes back after 19 years**
	USSR tested a hydrogen bomb
September	**Cane sugar rationing ended**

October	**The first commercial computer with rapid access memory went on sale**
November	*Panorama* first broadcast on BBC TV
	For the first time in 90 years England lost a Wembley football match against an overseas team (Hungary)
December	Float glass was patented by Pilkingtons
	Playboy Magazine was launched

Queen Elizabeth II dressed for her coronation, June 2, with the Duke of Edinburgh.

No sleep on the Mall

Betty Dawson

The year 1953 year was memorable to me for two reasons, one happy, one sad. In June my parents allowed me and my cousin with four of her friends from the Trings Royal Ballet School to go to London to watch the procession for the coronation of our Queen. We arrived at noon the day before and staked our place at the front of the pavement on the Mall. It was cold and raining, but we had waterproofs, food, blankets and everything to keep us warm and dry. Quickly the pavement filled up with happy people, who all talked to each other and lent or borrowed things. It was an incredibly happy place to be.

As the night drew on we all tried to sleep but there was always something to catch our interest, and the rain of course came down. Then suddenly we heard by bush telegraph that Edmund Hillary and his guide Tenzing had climbed Everest, the first people to achieve this. It seemed a good omen for our Queen and the shouting and singing started again. At last dawn broke. We got up and ate some breakfast. Someone came by selling hot tea from large jugs, as they walked down the street.

Betty's copy of the 2s 6d souvenir programme.

The police and soldiers then took their

143

positions lining the route. We had a very cheerful policeman who checked us all out as to where we were from and so on. Then at last the pageant began, but so did the rain again. The carriages holding VIPs and guests made their way to Westminster Abbey, led by the Lord Mayor magnificent in his robes. The noise got louder and just after 10am our young Queen and Philip arrived in the ornate golden state coach and the noise rose in a crescendo to a climax. She looked so beautiful in a dress the likes of which we had never seen. She was guarded by her Beefeaters in their glorious red uniforms. After this it went very quiet as everyone was listening to their radios. Then suddenly we heard the shout 'God Save the Queen' as the Queen was crowned. This was copied by the people in the street like a Mexican wave, and all the guns in Hyde Park were fired.

Eventually the royal couple returned, the Queen with the wonderful crown on her head. This time she was in a glass coach, so we all could see her and cheer loudly as she smiled and waved at us. This was followed by ladies-in-waiting and guests in truly lovely clothes – and more rain came too. Just as we were beginning to feel wet and cold, along came an open carriage surrounded by men in bare feet and straw skirts, no-one had seen the likes of. In the carriage were two robust figures, who turned out to be the Queen of Tonga and her son. She was as excited as we were, and was actually standing up in her open horse-drawn carriage in all the rain waving at us. She looked so joyful, that we all gave her such a cheer in return. Gradually

Side-cars for motorbikes were popular in the 1930s, 1940s and 1950s. Above is a 1951 motorbike and sidecar used by the AA for carrying repair equipment.

we made our way back to our aunt's house, wet, tired but so pleased we had been to London to see our Queen.

My second and sad memory of 1953 is about motor bikes and is a contrast to that happy day. My father was a very clever mechanic and built me a motorbike for my sixteenth birthday. He used to ride in trials and because he had a badly ulcerated leg which never got better (there was no penicillin then) he bought a side-car.

When my brother was called up I took his place in the side-car, which was fun. It was also sometimes dangerous. Once we toppled over on a steep hill and I was trapped under the bike which caught fire. Luckily I was able to escape, but minus eyebrows and fringe – all in the day's enjoyment. I rode well and was better than my brother, which caused problems when he was demobbed.

Unfortunately six months later my father, riding his motorbike, was killed by a drunken driver. The driver was taken to court and was the first man in England to be charged and found guilty of manslaughter in a traffic accident.

Coronation excitement

Lesley Wheeler

In 1953 I was six and the Coronation of our beautiful young Princess Elizabeth was announced. The death of her father the year before was curiously intertwined with the death of my grandfather. I had known Grandad was ill but was not allowed to see him or go to the funeral so I had to manage with memories of my occasional visits 'up north', and keep the sixpence he had given me in my treasure-box.

The achievement of Sir Edmund Hillary and Sherpa Tensing in conquering Mount Everest helped to build up the joy in the media and the public mind. My Dad had gone on a coastal tramp steamer to Scotland from Chatham when he was 17 and knew all about mountains. I had climbed Cat Bells and Snowdon so I knew lots too.

In the weeks before the Coronation all the children had been given Coronation mugs, some in bone china (*see below*). My parents had bought Coronation silver crowns in beautiful blue velvet boxes for the three of us to treasure, and we even had a small gold Coronation coach-and-horses which was '*not a toy*'.

The excitement at home built up even more when Dad decided to build a four foot high gold crown with ribbons, flags and a special banner which was to be sited on top of the porch. Whether he climbed out of my sister's bedroom window or went up a ladder I can't remember, but I was very proud to be part of such a loyal and clever family and I am sure I must have helped in some way or other.

On the morning of the Coronation, we all got up very early (so early that we saw the milkman and his horse-drawn cart) and had to flag down the bus as it was between stops. It was called the 'milk bus' by my mother as it was the first one on the run. It was going to Wembley Park and from there the underground tube trains were running specially for all the crowds that were expected.

Somehow we got to the Mall where there were people that had slept all night in Green Park. We saw special scaffolding stands that had been erected for VIPs, a few policemen and other groups and families who had started to arrive by 8 o'clock. We picked our spot, but of course the crowds swelled and our chances of seeing anything receded. We waited a long time and played games like *I Spy with my Little Eye* and alphabet games. Ever inventive and thinking ahead, Dad found a crate and two milk bottles for big sister to stand on, and I was promised a 'high horsey' on his shoulders, not just a piggy-back. Jon was told to find the biggest, burliest policeman lining the Mall to stand beside, and get there between the legs of those in front of us. We all had flags at the ready. Mum even had a flask of tea and some jam doughnuts at the ready.

The soldiers and string of carriages eventually came along, white horses on the Coronation coach I remember, and everyone waving and cheering. We got even hungrier waiting for the procession to come back again, with all the mounted cavalry soldiers, plumes bouncing, and this time we could shout 'God bless the Queen!' Jon got a good view, and so did the policemen lining the road. I saw it and could tell everyone at school I was really there, not just watching on the telly.

Coronation treat

Mary Dodds

In 1953, the year of the Queen's Coronation, the Admiralty, which sponsored the Community Centre I had joined, funded a trip to London for a group of us to go to see the Coronation. I was one of those chosen to go and stay for a few days as guests of the Admiralty. We stayed in a hotel in Buckingham Palace Road, were taken to Admiralty House and allowed to sit in Samuel Pepys' chair. It was at a large table that had had a semicircle cut out of it to accommodate Pepys' large tum. We were given a tour of the Admiralty and taken on a river cruise.

On the day of the Coronation, it drizzled and, after breakfast, we were taken to stands set up near Buckingham Palace. We had a good view as we were on the highest tier of the stand. We saw the Queen leave Buckingham Palace and then had to wait for what seemed hours (while we ate damp sandwiches) till she returned in the wonderful gold carriage wearing her crown and robes and carrying the Orb and Sceptre. She was accompanied by Prince Philip who waved to all the crowd.

The rain didn't put us off as we were so excited to be there amongst the pomp and pageantry. The crowds laughed and sang and waved flags, cheering at anything that went down the Mall, even the man who cleaned up after the horses of the cavalry.

Coronation anti-climax

Trish Kent

It was June 1953 and my world was just about to undergo a momentous change. The Coronation of Queen Elizabeth was to be seen throughout the world on television and I was going to watch it with my parents and brothers at Aunty Trippy's house along with about a dozen other people and children. The bunting was hung and even the street looked happy. We put on our party clothes and bright and early set off for the day. The living room had been totally rearranged so that,

Trish's Coronation scrap book.

A picture from Trish's scrap book of Princess Margaret with a cigarette holder. Both she and her father King George VI died of lung cancer attributed to smoking.

with the children on the floor and the adults on chairs, we could all see the nine inch screen which flickered as the valves warmed up. The highlight of the day was to be our Coronation tea, at which many delicacies had been promised, and the whole day to be completed with the cutting of the *ice cream cake,* something which we had never tasted and was reputed to be absolutely delicious.

The ceremony seemed to go on for ever and the boys soon got up and went outside to play Cowboys and Indians. As a girl I just wanted to see the new Queen's dress and whether Prince Charles and Princess Anne would attend (she stayed at home).

Finally tea arrived: plates full of sandwiches, fairy cakes, a Fullers coffee walnut cake and of course jelly. When we had worked our way through that we waited with baited breath for the ice cream cake. It was carried in with due ceremony. The red, white and blue icing was finished off with a ribbon of the same colours. The cake knife was produced and the cake cut. Portions were placed on fresh plates and I finally received my slice.

Tension was palpable as I bit into it - Ugh, Ugh, Ugh - it was revolting - layers of sponge cake with layers of what can only be described as very cold cardboard! It took me over ten years before I could bring myself to eat ice cream again and even today it has to be soft.

Coronation baby

Irene Taylor

The year 1953 was a memorable and exciting one for Britain. Memories of the war were receding and there was a new optimism and pride in the country's achievements. Mount Everest was conquered, England won The Ashes for the first time in 19 years, Queen Elizabeth II was crowned and, last but not least, my first child was born.

I had worked for nine years with the Inland Revenue but in accordance with Civil Service regulations had to relinquish my established post on marriage. I was able to continue on the same grade, albeit on a temporary basis, but with no pension accruing and no entitlement to maternity leave, such was the discrimination against married women in the workplace at that time. When I was six months pregnant, however, I resigned my post.

I enjoyed a relatively straightforward pregnancy, regularly attended ante-natal classes, drank copious amounts of orange juice (provided free to pregnant women) and ate lots of white cabbage to satisfy my craving.

We were strongly advised to have our first child in hospital, so when the time came I was duly admitted to GB Hunter Memorial Hospital (named after the Wallsend ship-builder) accompanied by my husband at around 10pm. I was nervous but excited at the prospect of becoming a mother, but came down to earth with a bump, so to speak, when greeted by a stern-faced unsympathetic midwife: she had seen it all before. After an initial examination, we were informed that the baby would not be born for several hours and my husband was sent home. Husbands were very much frowned upon by midwives in those days, and were certainly not allowed to be with their wives during labour or present at the birth.

I spent a long and frightening night on my own in a small room with no nurses in attendance and only the cockroaches scurrying around the edge of the floor for company. It was an old building dating from the early 19th century and in need of some refurbishment. The midwife reappeared at 7am and after further examination I was taken to the delivery room. It's best we draw a veil over the next few hours, but my labour eventually came to its inevitable conclusion. This was despite my having tried to make a bargain with God explaining that I had made a big mistake and would He please reverse the process after which I would enter a convent and lead a celibate life while devoting my time to doing good works. It was the 25th May which fell on Whit Monday that year (a good omen?) and just eight days before the coronation. I was now the mother of a bouncing baby boy weighing in at 6½ pounds and justifiably proud of myself. Babies were cared for in the nursery except at feeding times and visiting times. The latter were restricted to one hour each evening for husbands only. In those unenlightened times the lying-in period was ten days, so I was still in hospital for the Coronation and along with the other mothers allowed to watch the whole spectacle on a large TV screen in the day room. I was the envy of all my friends and relatives, none of whom owned a TV set at that time.

All the babies who were in the hospital on Coronation Day were presented with a souvenir silver spoon engraved with the Queen's head and the year, so my son can truly claim to be 'born with a silver spoon in his mouth'. To my shame I later lost the spoon, or thought I had until a few months ago when my son, now aged 57, came across it in a cutlery drawer. It's somewhat tarnished but I shall now restore it to its former pristine condition and put it on display in the china cabinet where it belongs.

The joy of bringing the baby home was soon overtaken by the exhausting routine that followed. The early part of the morning

The silver Coronation spoon given to Irene's new baby and now polished.

was taken up with lighting the coal fire, bathing and feeding the baby and tackling large piles of washing by hand. Nappies had to be boiled in a pail on top of the gas cooker, passed through a hand wringer and, weather permitting, hung out to blow on the line. The rest of the morning was taken up with the usual household chores but without the labour-saving appliances taken for granted today.

Food shopping was done daily as we had no fridge or freezer, so most afternoons involved a trip to the local shops with baby in his high Silver Cross pram (third hand but in mint condition) warmly wrapped in his pram rug – woven at Otterburn Mill in Northumberland. Neighbours would stop to admire the new-born and invariably produce a silver coin to put in his hand for luck, so progress was slow.

Christenings were quite low-key affairs in those days with the emphasis on the religious significance. My husband and I with the godparents walked to the nearby church for the short baptismal service. The christening gown was over 100 years old, beautifully made with intricate stitching. It had been handed down through several generations of my father's family. On the way to the church it was the tradition to present the first

Sketch on a 1950s skein of bias binding.

person you met of the opposite sex to the baby with a Christening Piece, usually a piece of christening cake and a silver sixpence. The recipient on this occasion was the young daughter of a neighbour who, by a happy coincidence, was standing by the gate as we left the house.

Back in the 50s, caring for babies was considered to be the woman's domain and, although proud to become a father, no self-respecting male (especially in the North East) would be caught washing nappies or walking out with the pram. And so it fell to the grandmothers and neighbours to provide the practical help and support during the first few months of a child's life. Neighbours with older children would give valuable advice and would pass on outgrown clothes, which were gratefully accepted. Cots, push-chairs and high chairs were also re-cycled, our high chair having given sterling service to my mother-in-law's six children. It was often a struggle to maintain the household on one income. Wages were paid in cash on a Friday and needed careful planning to last till the next pay-day.

A visit to the local cinema was the highlight of the week. We were enthralled by the big lavish Hollywood musicals with stars such as Judy Garland and Audrey Hepburn. Kitchen-sink dramas were not popular.

Things are very different today. Decrepit maternity hospitals have been replaced by clean and cheerful maternity wards in up-to-date hospitals with modern facilities and well-trained staff. Husbands (and partners, I hasten to add) are not only encouraged but even expected to be present at the birth (whether they like it or not, some might say). Babies now stay with their mothers on the ward and visiting times are much more flexible. Pregnant women have scans to monitor the progress of the unborn child, and it is even possible to find out the sex - so no surprises there then. Mothers and babies are usually discharged within 48 hours and mothers and fathers are entitled to share leave from work during the first important year.

Central heating, electric washers and driers and disposable nappies all help to lighten the workload, while shopping can be done on a weekly basis and stored in fridges and freezers. Women can now take a break from their careers with generous maternity leave and are able to return to work with the help of child-minders and nursery provision. Partners are more willing to accept their share of responsibility and roles are much more interchangeable, with fathers taking a greater interest in their children's upbringing. Women today are more liberated and able to choose how to manage their lives, plan their families and hopefully maintain a balance between career and motherhood. In retrospect, however, I am now glad that there was no pressure on mothers to return to the workplace when bringing up a family in the 50s, and that I was able to enjoy the precious pre-school years without feeling any guilt or regret.

1954

January	Comet airliner crashed in the Mediterranean, killing 35; accident attributed to metal fatigue
	Minus 66 degrees centigrade in Greenland
February	UK Atomic Energy Authority founded
	British Medical Committee reported a link between smoking and lung cancer
	First mass vaccination against polio in USA
	Queen Elizabeth made the first royal state visit to Australia
March	Lord Montague of Beaulieu, Peter Wildeblood and Michael Pitt-Rivers imprisoned for homosexual acts
April	BBC TV broadcast its first soap opera *The Grove Family*
	First motorway opened, Holland
	President Eisenhower's 'domino theory' speech, supporting intervention against communism
May	**Roger Bannister became the first person to run a four-minute mile**
	Zatopek ran 6 miles in 27.59 minutes
	US declared racially segregated schools to be unconstitutional
June	Eclipse of the sun visible in UK
	Alan Turing, code-breaker and computing genius, committed suicide after 'chemical castration' as a 'cure' for homosexuality
July	**Meat rationing ended, thus ending all wartime rationing**
	Denis Compton scored 278 runs in 290 minutes against Pakistan cricket team

	Armistice in Vietnam split the country into North and South
	First news broadcast on BBC TV
August	Maiden flight of first supersonic fighter plane, English Electric Lightning
October	Chris Chataway broke the world record for 500 metres by five seconds
	Britain ended its occupation of the Suez Canal
	The Allies ended the occupation of Germany
	The first transistor radio went on sale, Texas Instruments
	Dock workers' strike in England lasted into November
	The Viet Minh took control of North Vietnam
November	President Eisenhower offered help to South Vietnam
	First radio broadcast of *Hancock's Half Hour*
	BBC TV broadcast *Fabian of the Yard*, the first British police series
December	**First human kidney transplant, Boston USA**
	Winston Churchill became the first Prime Minister to reach age 80 in office

1954: the Regency TR-1, the first transistor radio.

The English Electric Lightning supersonic fighter, which first broke the sound barrier in 1954 (this photo was taken in 1964).

The last ration book

Kathy Ellis

By July 1954 rationing had ended, although the 1953-4 ration book included a page to apply for a new one. These are some of the 26 pages in my husband's last ration book for meat, eggs, fats, cheese, sugar, bacon and tea. Coal had also been rationed, and we had to register with a coal merchant. The registration certificate was posted to us in 1950 with a red 1d stamp, showing the king's head.

Needs of a growing family

Bessie Walshaw

In the early 1950s not many families were fortunate enough to own a television set. My Auntie Mollie ran a boarding house in Southport, while Uncle Willie earned money by tuning pianos and assembling them (my sister still has the baby grand he renovated). Their joint income enabled them to buy a (black and white) television set. They kept it in the back room away from the boarders' sight. It was also, as was a style then, set in a wooden cupboard with respectfully polished doors. The small size of the screen together with the doors made it rather difficult for several people to view together. Nevertheless we felt it worthwhile to travel the distance from Bradford where we lived to Southport to have a chance to watch the Coronation on TV. This was despite our having at that time a two-year-old daughter and my being heavily pregnant with our second. We were somewhat daunted to see that Auntie Mollie had invited several neighbours in to watch the event also. She had, however, prepared a lot of sandwiches and scones so that there would be no interruptions to the programme. Despite our

A 1950s version of a buggy for Bessie and her first four children

difficulties in actually seeing the screen it was a momentous occasion.

It was some years before my husband and I were able to consider affording a TV set, as our first two children were followed by five more. Ernest was a temporary clerk with the Inland Revenue after leaving the Forces, and as we had quite a large garden behind our house we decided to use it to add to our income. As our family grew we converted it into a mini garden centre.

We kept Rhode Island Red hens and others in two large sheds to supply us with eggs which we sold on Fridays on our 'egg round'.

The productive back garden.

At Christmas time we fattened cockerels for the table and I had to pluck and dress them. I used any broken or surplus eggs to make sponge cakes for sale in which the sandwich layer was our own home-made jam. The children were not enthusiastic about their share in collecting the eggs or in helping to clean out the sheds. We bred budgies (my older son's particular venture), although we had to stop when someone stole them. From our three greenhouses we had good crops of tomatoes which I used to make pickles. We sold seeds and bedding plants, as well as garden vegetables. Rhubarb was a popular item, too, which I sold very cheaply compared with the prices for forced early rhubarb today - I'm amazed at the price supermarkets charge now. We converted our back porch into a tiny shop, usually full of egg trays. The sale of puppies from our Jack Russell also helped us to make ends meet.

To help us with our 'business', Ernest bought a small van. A van was taxed more cheaply than a car, as long as windows were not installed in it. The children sat on cushions in the back, with the youngest on my knee – no seat-belts then. We used the van for delivering eggs, collecting chicken food, buying day-old chicks etc.

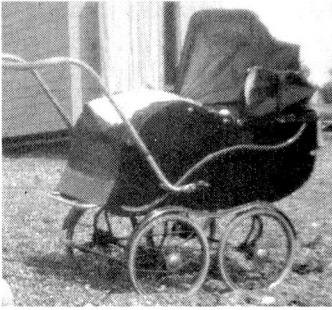

Another option for a growing family in the 1950s was Bessie's pram with a seat across the front; in those days very few men felt it was acceptable to be seen pushing a pram or pushchair.

It seemed sensible that I should to learn to drive, too. As at the time I was heavily pregnant with my sixth child (another one followed later), it was rather urgent that I should pass the driving test while I could find room to sit behind the steering wheel. Driving tests were simpler then than they are now; there was no theory part, nor motorways, and the test simply consisted of driving around, doing three-part turns and reversing. Fortunately I passed the test first time.

A way of saving money was to do one's own shoe repairs. Leather shoes frequently wore into holes but could be repaired at home with metal segs or leather if you had a cobbler's last (see right). The last has an arm for a large shoe at the top, one for a child's shoe at the left and one for the heel at the right.

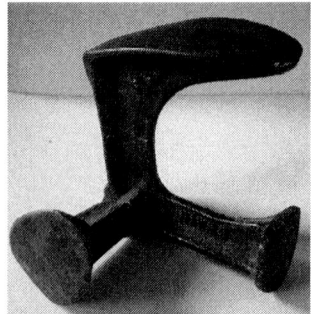

In the service of the Queen

Brian Cryer

Sixty years ago I received a letter in the name of the newly crowned Queen inviting me to help to defend the realm for a period of two years – yes, National Service. Although Yorkshire was my home county I was temporarily working in Newcastle and so had to report to the Oxford Salesrooms premises in New Bridge Street and signed up for the Royal Air Force. Eventually a travel permit came to get me to Padgate in Lancashire together with a 4/- postal order for the first day's pay (I still have it). Arriving at Padgate with about 200 others we were herded into groups of twenty in wooden huts and introduced to a little corporal I shall call Clinker whose sole purpose in life was to mould us into airmen in eight weeks by the most unpleasant way possible.

Next morning was uniform day. In a long queue we moved along a longer counter, first thrown a kit bag, then every item of uniform from hat to boots based on our height. No complaints were allowed. If it didn't fit you were deformed. Finally a long service number was stamped on everything and the kit bag filled. Then back to the hut to lay everything neatly out on the mattress for a kit inspection.

The next few days were a blurred memory of marching round a big square, runs to break in the boots and lectures to explain why we were lower life than worms and a disgrace to the Queen. One poor lad asked why they didn't let us go home if we were so bad. When the speechless corporal recovered he appointed the lad his messenger and kept sending him with messages to the other side of the camp. On his return he sent him back for a reply.

We were shown how to salute, and soon learned that if it moved you saluted it and if it was still you lined it up and painted it white. The hut had a single coke stove in the centre for heat with a box alongside for the coke. However the top layer was painted white for inspections and the coke to actually burn was brought from the outside pile as needed.

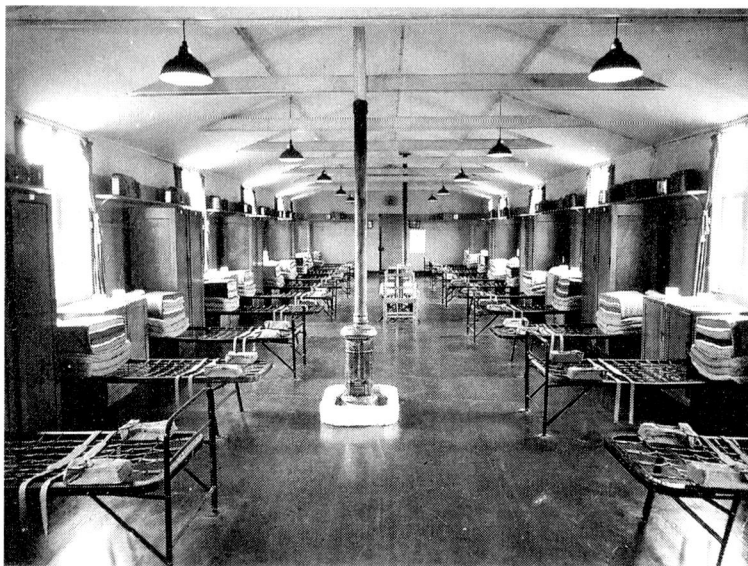

How Brian and his fellow soldiers had to leave their billet every morning, with bedding and equipment placed across their beds. Note the coke stove in the middle providing truly central heating.

On reflection the food wasn't bad: three cooked meals a day with bread-and-butter pudding the highlight. All left-over bread was collected for the week and made into the pudding. Any piece picked up off the floor with a heel mark in it was used to decorate the top. Any complainant was made chief bread picker-up for the week. The washhouse was adequate unless we upset the screaming corporal because he would then turn off the hot water. Each morning he ran cotton wool across our faces to ensure that we had shaved. We got our own back when his cold water failed for cooling his bath. He ordered us to use the water in the fire buckets

NAAFIs (Navy, Army and Air Force Institutes) were used for meals and entertainment. The chimney of the coke stove is visible centre left.

to cool his bath. We forgot (?!) that some people used the fire buckets if they were taken short in the night. Rifle drill was hard using the old Lee Enfield 303 rifles, not the pea shooters used today. We even did Military Funeral Drill - hopefully for Corporal Clinker. We weren't considered fit to go out of camp for the eight weeks and so the NAAFI was the main source of entertainment. The dartboard had no centre, but that didn't matter as we had no darts. The snooker table had balls but only half a cloth. Still the tea – there was no coffee - was hot, and the rock buns lived up to their name. Our immune system was tested with three jabs in one day, each at the end of a long queue. This was treated as a parade and therefore if you fainted it was an offence. Our little corporal gave us rifle drill after each jab 'to circulate the life blood', he said, the sadist. After eight weeks we were considered fit to be shown to the public at a passing out parade with full ceremony and band. Finally we were given our postings - me to RAF Church Lawford near Rugby as an instructor in the Airfield Construction Branch.

At the time National Service seemed an unnecessary break in my life and a waste of time, but on reflection I learned a lot about life: working together, don't let the ******s grind you down, respect your superiors by rank not necessarily by person, make the best of the situation and *never volunteer*. Alright, I forgot some, or I would never have been Chairman of Newcastle U3A.

Transatlantic sea, land and air

June Thexton

During WW2 personal travel had been very restricted. Petrol was rationed across the board and car owners got very little unless they offered to transport others eg to hospital. I remember my uncle who did this saying, when giving us a surreptitious lift to a local beauty spot: 'Try not to look as if you're enjoying yourselves!'

1954: The Empress of Australia liner.

and (below) its "First class Room 41 with private bath and toilet"; today, of course, most cabins are 'en suite'.

Trains were often requisitioned to carry troops and vital supplies, so ordinary folk in my part of the world, Barrow-in-Furness, cycled or relied on the buses, usually crowded, smoky and clapped -out.

By the fifties, a start had been made on renewing the ageing rolling stock and vehicles, but if people had cars at all, they tended to be pre-war bangers constantly needing attention. When I got my driving licence, the first thing I learned was how to change a wheel: tyres were a constant problem. Foreign travel for the masses was still a long way off and cheap flights unheard of.

It was against this background that, in September 1954, I found myself embarking on the Canadian Pacific liner, the Empress of Australia, recently refitted from being a troop ship, at Liverpool's Albert Dock. The city had no hints of future cultural splendours then, and the dock had all the grime and tackle needed by a working port. I had been fortunate enough to be awarded a Rotary Foundation Research fellowship to study abroad and was en route to McGill University in Montreal.

CANADIAN PACIFIC STEAMSHIPS LIMITED
EMPRESS OF AUSTRALIA
(Captain J. DOBSON D.S.C., R.D., R.N.R.)

- ABSTRACT OF LOG -

LIVERPOOL to QUEBEC and MONTREAL   SAILED SEPTEMBER 3rd 1954.

Distance -- Liverpool to Montreal 2,756 miles.

Date	Lat. N.	Long. W.	Dist.	Wind	Force	Weather, Remarks, Etc.
Sept. 3	Stage to	Bar Lt.vsl	16	W	5-6	4.45 p.m. Left Princes Landing Stage
						6.17 p.m. Pilot left. 6.18 p.m. dep. from Bar Lt. Vsl.
,, 4	55.49	9.48	284	W to S	7-4	5.50 a.m. Inishtrahull
						Rough to mod. sea, Cloudy and clear.
,, 5	56.30	21.17	380	Var	4-6	Rough sea, mod. swell. O'cast, Occ'l rain.
,, 6	56.03	32.32	375	NW-NE	5-2	Mod. sea and swell. Cloudy and clear. occ'l rain
,, 7	54.45	43 29	381	N-ESE	4-7	Mod. to rough sea, moderate heavy swell
						O'cast and clear. Occ'l rain.
,, 8	52.23	53.21	378	WNW	3-7	Mod. to rough sea, mod. swell, Cloudy and clear.
						5.09 p.m.Belle Isle.
,, 9	50.00	62.31	386	W'ly	2	Slight sea, Fine and clear.
,, 10	To	Father Pt.	259	SSW	3	4.12 a.m. arr. off Father Point 4.32 a.m. pilot boarded
						4.41 a.m. left Father Point.
,, 10	Father Pt.	to Quebec	158			Expect to arrive at Quebec at 3.30 p.m.
,, 11	Quebec to	Montreal	139			Expect to arrive at Montreal at 9.30 a.m.

BEAUFORT WIND SCALE.—0 Calm.   1 Light Air.   2 Light Breeze.   3 Gentle Breeze.   4 Moderate Breeze.   5 Fresh Breeze.
6 Strong Breeze.   7 Moderate Gale.   8 Fresh Gale.   9 Strong Gale.   10 Whole Gale.   11 Storm.   12 Hurricane.

F. Granger, R.D., R.N.R., Chief Officer.   W. Elliot, Chief Engineer.
Dr. M. Bowen, M. B., Ch.B. Surgeon.   F. C. Talbert, Purser.   F. Benson, Chief Steward.

The ship's log for June's voyage bears testimony to the weather.

The ten-day journey proved an eye opener for me, if a rather scary one. I had no idea what to expect. The passengers were a mixed bunch of wealthy US and Canadian visitors, business people, and family members joining others who had already emigrated, but there were few tourists as we think of them. The food and drink on offer was abundant and sumptuous, as it was going to be in Canada, by our just-post-rationing standards. The weather offered everything the North Atlantic could provide in autumn: fierce gales round the north of Ireland (no stabilisers then), calm stretches with icebergs off Greenland, and wastes of grey water and sky on the St. Lawrence River when we arrived in what seemed no-man's land as we couldn't see the banks of the river for about two days.

I was greeted with what I came to realise as typical warmth and interest by the mainly English-speaking Rotarians. I soon became accustomed to their large posh cars with ample 'gas'. I saw their Cadillacs and Buicks with their front bench seats, on-the-wheel gearsticks and interiors so luxurious compared to our family's tiny utility Ford Anglia. As I got into my University work, of course, I returned to my usual forms of student transport - Shank's pony and the bus, snow permitting. I remember waiting for a rural bus in a quiet little town up-river in 20° below, wondering if I would turn to an ice statue if it didn't come soon.

During my time there, I made a few train journeys too - not transcontinental ones, but to relatives in North Bay, Ontario, for Christmas. The train ploughed for hours through the interminable pine forests past the mysterious radio-active cobalt mines.

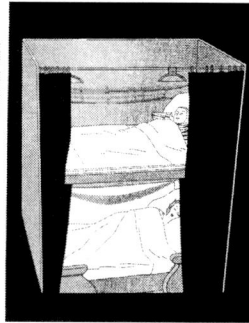

1954 Sleeping Car accommodation on Canadian Pacific trains could be luxurious: one option, if the 'standard' version above was not good enough, was The Drawing Room with sofa berths and separate private toilet facilities.

For New Year I went to Lake Erie. The US Customs came on the train and made everyone turn out their liquor supplies, but not before some serious seasonal attempts to dispose of them. Our Hall of Residence in Montreal was up the hill from the main marshalling yards and the mournful cries of the railway diesels haunted the peaceful nights - never to be forgotten.

166

During my study time I had the commitment to visit many Rotary Clubs to talk about life in the UK, my research etc. Rotary had an all-male membership in those days and the big city clubs had over 400 members, which made for quite a daunting audience. Smaller clubs, often French Canadian, were more homely, held in village halls decorated with moose-heads and hunting guns. Of course I got lifts to these venues in all kinds of vehicles complete with entertaining company. I never did get used to the vast spaces between locations even in eastern Canada.

When the University course finished, some of us were keen to apply to drive new vehicles from Detroit out west, a common means of travel for students to see other parts. Disappointingly the scheme terminated that year and we hadn't money for the Greyhound busses. Instead Rotary helped me to plan a farewell tour of clubs in Nova Scotia, New Brunswick and New England. This involved me in the first flight I ever took. It was from Halifax to Boston in a converted Pioneer – exciting in all respects, as it was small, basic and bouncy. It was common then for ex-war planes to be reconditioned for the commercial market.

Eventually my travels took me to New York and one of the best and cheapest rides in the world. It was on a boat round Manhattan Island from which you could see the down-and-outs living in cardboard boxes on the dockside under the towering splendour of the Wall Street banks. It probably gave me the sort of social jolt I needed to get interested in politics. Another eye-opener was the overhead railway, seen in so many films, which took you from the wealth of Fifth Avenue through the migrant and black districts. In my case this was to see the New York Giants playing. I still have the ticket (*see right*).

RAIN CHECK *

GAME NO. 23

02592

GRAND STAND ADMISSION
Est. Price $1.13
Fed. Tax .11 TOTAL $1.30
N. Y. C. Tax .06

NEW YORK GIANTS
BASEBALL CLUB
POLO GROUNDS

In the event that 4½ innings of this game are not played, this coupon will be good for any subsequent championship game during this season and may be exchanged at Box Office for this priced ticket.

Horace C. Stoneham President

See Other Side For Conditions

I was due to return to the UK on the Mauretania from New York in June 1955, so I was horrified to read in the paper that a massive dock strike at home meant that it – and I – wouldn't be sailing. I was down to my last few dollars and hadn't thought to apply for a work passport. I'd already had to sign a statement that I wasn't a member of the Communist Party to get a visa, this being the McCarthy era.

So I had to re-establish contact with Rotary and ask for help. I was lucky enough to have got friendly with some ex-pat Yorkshire folk in Rhode Island who invited me to stay until I could get alternative transport. It finally materialised as a horrendously expensive flight via BOAC (I did manage to get re-embursed for it eventually) and came home on the latest Stratocruiser. This was a double-decker state-of-the-art plane with a full-sized bar and a spiral staircase. My first transatlantic flight proved memorable. In those days all these flights had to refuel en route. The first stop was at Ganda in Newfoundland, where we

The Boeing B377 Stratocruiser arriving at Heathrow, September 12 1954.

got out into a huge hangar in the cold mist of dawn; the second was Prestwick when I seem to remember we had lunch – all very leisurely. We finally arrived at Heathrow passenger terminal, then a smallish building a bit like a glorified cricket hut in the middle of a field. It was much to the relief of my family.

So, back to reality.

These were the times when transatlantic culture fascinated those of us still emerging from wartime restrictions, and I had been lucky enough to see it at first hand. I had, of course, many other memories to conjure with as I rode my bike along the wind-swept north-west coast to my first teaching job.

A culture shock indeed!

168

1955

	Vietnam War began (ended in 1975)
January	The first of three train crashes with fatalities this year, at Sutton Coldfield, Milton and Barnes, total killed 41, injured 235
February	A big freeze across Britain
March	**Train engineers and firemen called a strike which led to a state of emergency in May and lasted until June 14**
April	End of a month-long strike of maintenance workers which prevented national newspapers being published
May	**Newcastle United won the FA Cup for the sixth time, with a 3-1 win over Manchester City**
	USSR and Eastern Bloc of European countries signed the Warsaw Pact
	Anthony Eden became Prime Minister
June	Children became protected from horror comics by the Children and Young Persons Act
July	**Bertrand Russell manifesto highlighted dangers of nuclear weapons, basis of the Campaign for Nuclear Disarmament**
	Ruth Ellis became the last woman to be hanged in the UK
	Stirling Moss became the first English winner of the British Grand Prix
August	First publication of *Guinness Book of Records*
	Heat wave and drought
September	For the first time the BBC TV showed newsreaders reading the news (Richard Baker,

	Kenneth Kendall)
	Airfix produced their first model aircraft kit
	ITV started broadcasting; first advertisement was for Gibbs SR toothpaste. The BBC countered by killing off Christine Archer on popular radio serial *The Archers*
	Fish fingers first sold in Britain, Birdseye
October	Princess Margaret called off her proposed marriage to divorced Peter Townsend
	Rosa Parks increased desegregation pressure in US by refusing to give up her bus seat for a white person
December	**Hovercraft design patented by Cockerell**

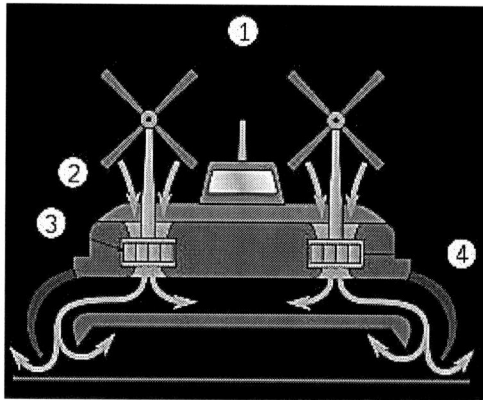

Hovercraft design showing how the propellers (1) send air (2) by means of the motors (3) to raise the flexible skirt (4) above the surface of the water.

The good life and nostalgic cars

Ruth Lesser

Newly married we moved to a village near Nottingham when my mother lent us the wherewithal to buy a small building that had been used as a weaving shed. Oddly all its windows were of frosted glass except the one where a toilet had been installed (echoes of my 1947 French experience there). It was on land behind the old manor house which itself had been converted into the Post Office, and with the shed came four acres in two fields. We agreed to continue the village tradition of allowing one of the fields to be used for the annual village fête.

We gradually made the shed habitable. One addition, which drew visitors from the village was the building of an outsize bath lined with black tiles. David was commuting to Nottingham daily (his

1955: The good life, with kid goats, geese and hens.

salary at Viyella was £500 a year), and I spent some of my time trying to realise our fantasy of having a smallholding. With my

171

French-learned milking skills, the British Alpine goats were no problem once we got an electric fence to keep them from wandering. We had hens, geese and ducks, and rented out part of the (non fête-dedicated) field to the local coalman for him to pasture his powerful cart-horse. The horse had a frightening way of charging across the field when he saw me crossing to the goat shed with a milking

David and guest John Newson starting on the chicken meal, watched with interest by bull mastiff Smith.

stool and bucket, and I feared he might be resentful that the latter didn't contain anything for him. Least successful were our attempts to grow vegetables. We neither of us relished digging into hard turf which had been uncultivated for many years, and David, who had been brought up in India with servants who tackled those sort of jobs, was not, so to speak, born with a spade in his hand. He did learn the art of breaking a chicken's neck, though, when we wanted one for the pot. I recall one occasion when we invited two of our university friends who had moved to Nottingham to come over for a chicken dinner. They were somewhat surprised to find that the visit started with the killing and plucking of the chicken.

We eventually succumbed to the advice of the pharmaceutical company which had sent me away at a job interview because newly married women should have

Two kids happy in a wheelbarrow.

172

babies. Our first son was born in 1955 in the living-room of the shed-house, to the accompaniment of a recitation of Dylan Thomas's *Under Milk Wood* on the wireless (it had made its debut the year before). The two midwives sat in the corner of the room, smoking and reading our Natural Childbirth book, the novelty of which intrigued them. The rule then was that all first babies (ie to primagravida) should be born in hospital. We had had quite a fight to be allowed to have our baby born at home, but David and I were determined that he should be there at the birth and it would not have been allowed in the hospital. I was also keen not to subject the baby to the 'gas and air' which was the usual painkiller used to help mothers in labour, whether they asked for it or not. My labours were long enough with all my five babies, but uncomplicated, and I managed to keep to the natural childbirth principles through all the deliveries.

It was the arrival of babies that made us think about transport. For the first two babies a second-hand Silver Cross pram did the job supplemented by a folding pushchair and carrying sling. When number three was on the way, I was going to need something else. In the village we had acquired a rather eccentric large car. It was ex-army and had been used in the war in North Africa. To

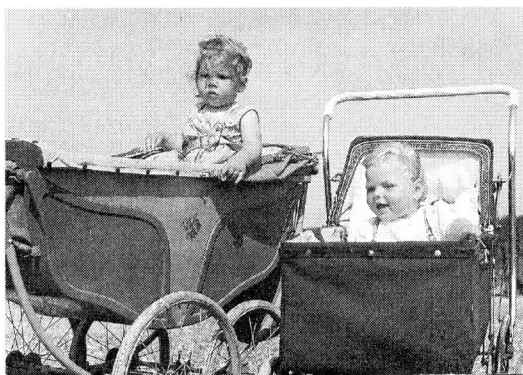

1950s Silver Cross prams were real, sturdy 'baby carriages', capable of carrying two sitting babies in style. Our pram was still in use in 1960 for one-year-old Juliet on the left (a pink transfer of a rose was applied to it for her as the first girl after three boys); her cousin Janet is on the right, as a visitor in a more versatile, removable, cloth carry-cot on a wheeled frame.

cope with the sandy terrain it had balloon tyres. The body was a sun-bleached pink with a wooden framing. The windscreen was hinged at the top and could be raised to allow guns to be inserted for firing above the dashboard. The downside, of course, was how to use the windscreen wiper, and it was fitted with a knob which the passenger could manipulate when the windscreen was lowered. Another, alas too fraught, eccentricity was that the accelerator pedal often stuck in the down position, leading to some skilled motoring to guide the vehicle to an upward slope where the handbrake could hold while the driver freed the cable. It got us to Felixstowe from Nottinghamshire when David changed his job, and ended its romantic life as a kennel for our beautiful, loyal bull mastiff, Smith.

Learning to drive in such a car was too much of a challenge for me, especially when pregnant, so we bought a little green Ford van. It had had windows inserted at the sides, which meant unfortunately that it was taxed at the higher rate as a car. It also had a slipping clutch, which involved keeping just the right level of acceleration if you were waiting at traffic lights going up a hill. David taught me to drive it (though we had some

The family's first Humber, with spare wheel on the roof, hidden wiper, AA badge and one-year-old Piers on the running board.

arguments about distinguishing 'left' and 'right') and I passed the test in it at the first attempt. There must have been some leniency from the driving test officer who saw the urgency of my condition, and who only drew to my attention the need not to cross my arms over the steering wheel in case any cuff studs I might be wearing (!) became entangled.

174

With the total demise of the Ford's clutch, we bought a blue Bedford van. This really was a *van* without side windows, and taxed as such, but came with its own challenges. It had no synchromesh on the gears, which meant gear-changing without grating was a delicate art – such satisfaction when I got it right by listening carefully for the right number of revs. It also had to be started on the handle. It is an art learning how to use a starting handle without risking breaking a thumb. Hill starts were another danger – it was important that the engine didn't stall as you would have had to get out to start it again – and the training on the Ford came in useful. The Bedford's fatal, final fault was the rusty holes in the floor at the driver's feet.

We had other nostalgic cars, all second-hand and bought in sequence on a small budget. The Lea Francis had a magnificent chrome radiator grill but a tired engine. The Humber Pullman Super Snipe was advertised as 'a fast gentleman's car' and David was tempted by the idea of becoming a fast gentleman.

We did most of our own repairs in our back yard, including changing the engine gasket, but spare parts were hard to get for the Humber Pullman and we had to search for them in the scrapyards. We eventually drove it with stateliness to the breaker's yard, where the yardman was glad to take it as 'there's a demand for parts for these'. We wondered if he had just lost his market.

The world of second-hand cars received a jolt in 1960 when the Ministry of Transport introduced its test, the 'MOT', and cars over 10 years old had to be checked for the efficiency of their brakes, lights and steering every year. I doubt if any of the cars we had driven before then would have passed – and we drove them without seat belts, too. The modern three-point retractable car–seat belt wasn't developed until 1952, but they didn't become compulsory, and then only for front seats, until the 1970s.

A child at the end of the Raj

Jennifer Ball

I was born in a hill station called Nainital in the Himalayas on the 22nd of October 1943, so, really, I was a child at the end of British Raj in India. I am the sixth generation from my mother's family to be born in India and my memories of my childhood are of a great deal of freedom and being very spoilt as an only child.

I spent most of my time with my *ayah*, Monka, and Indian servants as was the custom. Monka was, to me, very old, having been my mother's ayah too. It was the custom for generation after

Jennifer in Allabad with her parents, Monka and servants.

generation of Indian servants to stay with the same European family. I remember her as a little old lady, always in a white sari, but as my mother was 19 when I was born, she was probably not that old.

I did not see a great deal of my parents. My father was in the Indian Fire Service and had come out to India at the end of 1942. He was seconded to the Indian Fire Service from Manchester - I'm not sure why. My mother's family were what was known as 'Domiciled Europeans' and had been granted land in the District of Gorakhpur, about 70 miles from the border with Nepal. They were called *zemindars*, landowners who rented land to tenants for farming. The estate had been in the family since approximately 1859.

Netour Estate House.

We spent the winter months – say November to March or April - at the Estate House, known as Netour Estate. It was large with high ceilings. There were four bedrooms, each with a bathroom attached, a large dining room and a separate sitting room. A veranda ran around three sides of the house. There was no running water or electricity. Our water came from two wells and light was from oil lamps. There were also long fabric fans suspended from hooks in the ceilings and a *punka wallah* would sit outside the main rooms and pull the fan back and forth. A hole in the wall to the outside with a rope attached to the fan allowed him to sit and pull away, something that was normal in my life and taken for granted.

The kitchen was a separate building from the house with a raised and covered walkway. All the cooking was done by the cook and his assistants on a built-up, clay-type contraption with holes for the cooking pots and fired underneath with wood and charcoal. I grew up on Indian food, and even today my comfort food is *dhal* - spiced red lentils - and rice. I also love fresh *chapattis*, which I used to eat rolled up with butter dripping out of them.

We had an estate manager by the name of Lal Bahurdar, who managed the property when my parents were away over the hot season. Their house was about hundred yards from the 'Big House' and they had a daughter the same age as me. I spent many hours with her – her name is Santi – and also ate with them. However they were Brahmins, the highest caste in India, and I used to be given my food on a banana leaf so as not to contaminate their plates. I, of course, ate with my hands, was part of their family and they always treated me as such.

The grounds were enormous around Netour so we were self sufficient in vegetables, had two cows for milk, yoghurt and butter. Also there were numerous chickens and a couple of goats. I loved goats and had a small cart, like a miniature bullock cart, made for me which was pulled by two goats. Not too far from the house was the local bazaar

The 'bullock cart'.

and the butcher would lead live goats through a path near our house. If I saw them I would plead with my father to buy the goats and save them as they were slaughtered for meat. At one time we had quite a few goats as my father usually gave in to me.

The fields were ploughed using a wooden hand-plough pulled by bullocks which had a thin rope through their noses. There were usually two. When the wheat was ready it was separated from the stalks by being spread out on hard ground with two bullocks walking in circles over it again and again. It was then put into a flat woven basket and the chaff separated from the wheat by the wind.

Jennifer with friend Santi and rescued goat Modi and her kids.

I can remember going with my father on the back of his bicycle to collect the rents from our tenants in the villages. Chairs would be brought out and he would be seated with some ceremony whilst I went off to play with the children. If it was the time of the sugar cane harvest I would be given small brown balls made from the juice of the cane which had been boiled and then rolled. They were very sweet and sticky. The sugar-cane juice was extracted in the villages by a bullock going round and round a machine into which the cane was fed.

My life at Netour was special. I was about 12 years old when I was there for what turned out to be the last time although I was not told we would not return, and so did not have the opportunity to say goodbye to all of it.

In the hot season we lived in Nainital where my family also owned a house, named Arglesford, which had been bought by my grand father in the early 1920s. One of my earliest memories is of the journey from Netour to Nainital by train. The nearest station was three to four miles away and was named Campiergung, after my great-great-grandfather Campier, who had been given the Netour Estates in about 1858/59.

We would travel to the station in style from the Netour house by bullock cart. A special one had been constructed for the family's use with seats and high sides. Then we had about an hour-long train journey to the nearest large city, Gorakhpur. Next was an overnight train journey to Lucknow. The travelling compartments were private, and consisted of bunks made up with pristine sheets and a tiny washbasin and toilet. Tea was served in the early morning by a bearer (the Indian name for a steward) in an immaculate white uniform. We spent the whole day at the railway station in Lucknow, in the European Ladies Waiting Room, which had a bathroom and dining room. My mother would be there as well as my grandmother. My recollection is somewhat vague as to what we did all day but my ayah was always present too. In the evening we would set off for the last leg of the train journey, again with bunk beds, to the station nearest to Nainital, about 20 miles away, called Kathgodam.

From there we would complete the rest of the trip by car as the railway could not go any higher due to a steep winding road which at times was blocked by landslides. We probably had a couple of cars as there was always a large amount of luggage. This was carried by porters on their backs, with a headband across the forehead, up to our house set high on the hills overlooking the town and lake (the *tal* in Nainital means *lake* in Hindi). I have always loved train travel and put this down to my childhood.

The house at Nainital was set in large grounds, the front garden going down to the boundary in three terraces. Lots of flowers and vegetables were grown in the gardens at the side of the house. The climate was such that all types of vegetables flourished. The house consisted of a long veranda at the front with a sitting room and dining room behind. There were four bedrooms, two with dressing rooms and each with a bathroom and toilet. Here also we had electricity but no running water: there was one servant (of the lowest caste) whose only duty was to heat water and fill the tin baths in each bathroom and empty the toilet bowls. The latter were set into chairs with a hole for the bowl. Water was heated in a

Jennifer's parents at 'Arglesford', the house in Nainital.

large aluminium tank set on legs with a tap to let it out and a fire was lit underneath.

Age five in 1948, I started school in Nainital at St Mary's Convent run by a German order of nuns, which my mother had also attended. The school year ran from 6th of March to the 6th of December. From about the age of seven I was a boarder for March and April, then a day girl once my parents came up from the Netour Estate house until about the end of October: Most of the pupils were boarders, daughters of rich Indians and expatriates. We lived in large dormitories and had to attend chapel each morning for Mass, twice on Sundays.

As a day girl, since we lived about three or four miles from the school, I used to go to school on a horse, a lovely grey one. Nainital then had no traffic apart from a road around the lake so you either rode, walked or were carried in a sedan type chair known as a *dooley*. I mainly rode. The horse was brought up to the house each morning by its owner. I rode, the *syce* (stableman) ran behind and the process was repeated in the afternoon.

Until I started school I refused to speak English, always saying that I would when I went to school, which I did. My first language was Hindi.

There were four schools in Nainital: two Roman Catholic and two Church of England. The Catholic Boys school was called St. Joseph's and was next to the Convent. My parents were good friends with the Minister of the Church of England Boys' school, Sherwood College, and his wife. Their daughter was the same age as me, also called Jennifer, and we spend a lot of time together as families.

There were many places to picnic. The children would ride, and sometimes my mother would be carried in a dooley. Large hampers containing food, plates, cutlery etc would arrive at the picnic places before us and it would all be laid out, with the bearers waiting to serve the food. The picnic places had names like 'Tiffin Top' and 'Dorothy's seat'.

Games would be organised too. Once we found a monitor lizard. We also had two dogs at Nainital, a pedigree red setter named Rex and a small mongrel dog that had appeared and adopted the family. Rex was really my father's dog and when we left in 1956 to come to live in England he tried hard to bring Rex with us. I think it must have been too difficult, so I left behind something else which I loved.

At the Nainital house we had about 15 servants, overseen by a steward known as the 'Mate'. He organised the house, although my

182

mother would see the cook each morning to discuss the menu for the day and give out the supplies which she kept in a locked storeroom. Here too the kitchen was separate from the house and connected to it by a covered walkway.

We had two gardeners who grew lots of vegetables. The gardens at the side of the house were given over to vegetables and fruit trees: lemons, apricots, peaches. There was also the *dhobi* who was responsible for the washing and ironing. He used a hollow iron with a top which was filled with charcoal to heat it.

Everything was done for us. It was a life which I took for granted and did not give much thought to.

My grandmother, my mother's mother, had died just after my seventh birthday and surprisingly I don't really remember her although I spent most of my early years with her rather than my parents. She was only 64, but had been ill for some time and in the hospital at Nainital. I had been put into school as a boarder during this time and I can remember one of the nuns who looked after us taking me to the school infirmary and being told that my grandmother had died and then being taken to the chapel to pray for her soul. My only memory of her is of a really old lady too.

For a while we had two of my grandmother's sisters living with us at Nainital, Aunty Lily and Aunty Clare, both unmarried. They had also been born in India. I think my grandmother was one of about nine children. After Indian independence Aunty Clare went to live with another of her sisters in Glasgow, who must have married someone British. Aunty Lily died and was buried next to my grandmother at the Christian cemetery in Nainital. I remember that the two Aunts used to really annoy me as they seemed to walk around making little moaning noises all the time and yet Aunty Lily was only 62 when she died.

We left India in November 1956. Netour Estate which had been the family source of income was taken back by the Indian

Government in about 1952/53. I don't remember much about it except that all large landowners' estates were abolished and the land redistributed to the former tenants. My parents did receive compensation from the government but this is not something I remember much about.

Because my father was British we were able to come to England. My final memory of Nainital is leaving Arglesford on my favourite grey horse: the road from the house was quite steep and I turned around in the saddle looking back at the house for as long as I could. Even at that age I felt that I had to imprint the house and gardens in my head.

All the servants from the house accompanied us to the far end of the lake from where we left by car to travel to Kathgodam. Everyone was crying and garlands of marigolds were put around our necks. My mother in particular was very, very upset: after all we were going to a country which we did not know.

We travelled from Kathgodam to Cawnpore (now known as Kanpur), stayed with friends for a few days and then finally on to Bombay (now Mumbai) and then by ship to Liverpool. The Mate from Arglesford accompanied us to Bombay, as did the family lawyer who stood waving as the ship pulled away.

It was the end of my Indian childhood, one which I remember with great affection.

1956

	Rock and Roll became popular in Britain, as did coffee bars
January	Possession of heroin became illegal
February	The spies Burgess and Maclean reappeared in Moscow
	Double yellow parking lines introduced, Slough
April	**Premium Bonds introduced**
	A British jazz record made the top twenty, Lyttleton's *Bad Penny Blues*
May	Granada TV launched
	Minister of Health said ill effects of smoking had not been proven
	First British area designated as of Outstanding Natural Beauty, Gower Peninsula
June	Third Class on trains redesignated as Second Class
July	**Clean Air Act passed**
August	Police investigation of claims that society doctor John Bodkin Adams had murdered up to 400 patients
September	**Transatlantic telephone cable between the UK and North America inaugurated**
October	The Queen opened the world's first commercial nuclear power station at Calder Hall
November	**British and French seized control of two Suez Canal ports**
	Russians quelled with tanks an anti-communist uprising in Hungary
	Petrol rationing introduced following blockades due to Suez crisis (ends in May 1957)
December	British and French withdrew from Suez under UN pressure

War Department surplus

Bryan Cryer

For me as a budding electrical engineer, one of the good things to come out of the post war years was the amount of ex-War Department (WD) equipment that came on the market at a fraction of its original value. My local market at Doncaster had a stall that was piled high with everything that had been used in the war, and Johnny Burley who ran it could suggest a use for everything. Rumour had it that he could even get a tank at the right price.

I was less ambitious and my first purchase was a bomb-sight off a Lancaster bomber. Apart from the actual visual sight it was mounted on a frame full of interlinked gear wheels all connected to dials where you could set the height, range, wind and aircraft speed as well as bomb details. I had great fun aiming at local houses and setting all the 'necessary' parameters. The house of a local schoolteacher was a favourite target, but alas bombs were off the purchase list. Still, I had a good imagination, let down when I got to school the next day.

Eventually the gearwheels were cannibalised and added to the Meccano set that

A 1956 instruction book for Meccano, showing how to build a drag line excavator with the green and red pieces bolted together.

my father had handed down to me - I still have it.

About this time vinyl records were becoming more available and, since a commercial hi-fi was out of my price range, I decided to build one based on a circuit diagram in the Practical Wireless magazine. Back to the market for the parts: glass and metal valves the size of present day light bulbs, transformers the size of a box of chocolates and a large box of resistors, capacitors and connectors that finished up in my mother's vacuum cleaner for years afterwards. Everything was big. The days of freely available diodes, transistors and micro components were a long way off. It took a long time to build the unit and an even longer time to get it to work. A wrong component, wrong position or a badly made soldered joint produced either a screech, nothing or a blinding flash. A circuit correction in Practical Wireless several months later didn't help. The loudspeaker was 15 inches in diameter, probably from an airfield Tannoy system, and helped me to show the neighbours what 30 watts into a big speaker could do. The War Department did not seem to use record turntables and reluctantly I had to buy a new one. The cabinet came next, the size of a sideboard, and because of its size it had to be a piece of furniture. The unit was totally wood with the outside faced with figured oak ply which had hours of French polish lovingly rubbed into it. My arms ached for a long time afterwards. Perhaps this was responsible for my feelings for the French. I'm not sure that it wasn't this cabinet that attracted my future wife! Eventually I became more adventurous and added a radio tuner. Unfortunately it was never a success because ex WD tuner components were designed for receiving military wavelengths, not the BBC. The family claimed that the unit spent more time 'under modification' than actually working.

Fortunately commercial advances rescued me and good quality radio and record players came on the market at an affordable price. The home-made unit was abandoned. The components lay around for a while in the hope of reuse, but the cabinet finished its days as the most elegant rabbit hutch in the area. The reduction in the number of ex WD components coincided with the arrival of a family and no more similar major projects were attempted. However the experience of 'researching component availability' (always look for a bargain) never left me, and stood me in good stead when making caravans, forts, dolls' houses and model railways for the children. I still have a gas mask and steel helmet in the loft, and a garden shed and garage full of bits and pieces that 'will come in useful one day'.

I am pleased to be old enough to have lived through and remember the pioneering days, and getting something to work against all the odds and parental advice. The advent of the micro components used in i-Pods, computers, mobiles and printed circuits have robbed the youth of today of the joy of starting from scratch and using basic components to build up a project with the pleasure you experience if it works, and the urge to try again if it doesn't. It is not the same buying a finished item 'made in the Far East' for a few pounds even if it has a 99% chance of working first time. I still get a kick out of buying something and being able to take it back and say *'It does not work'*.

Choking on a Polo

Lesley Wheeler

The little newsagent and sweet shop outside the tube station and the tobacco and sweet kiosks on the London Underground platforms were beacons of indulgence to me as a ten-year-old. Several times a week I would have a few coppers to spend on my own choices. My parents regularly bought bags of sweets that were kept in the kitchen china cupboard, generally glacier mints or hard butter-scotch to unwrap and suck as a treat or to take on long car journeys to break up the monotony. On trips to Halifax to see my grandparents I would be offered humbugs, and there in the big heavy dresser would be a special tin of stripy mints or golden honey-coloured pyramids. Occasionally we had bars of chocolate in the house and if we had a family trip to 'the Pictures' or a London theatre often my mother would be bought a box of Black Magic and would try to unwrap the crinkly paper quietly.

Some sweet-shops had dozens of big glass jars of loose boiled sweets of all colours and shapes, and for a few pennies you could buy a paper bagful. In my London sweet-shop on the way home from school I would look longingly at the jars of pear drops, pineapple cubes, jelly babies and all-sorts, and if I had enough money I might buy a small bag of lemon sherbets that cracked open and fizzed in my mouth.

More often I would go for the cheap assortment down at hand-pick level, and get two fruit salads for a penny, sticky and chewy but wrapped in a small cube, or four black-jacks (liquorice tasting chews), also wrapped. I liked bags of sherbet dip with a dipper to lick up the powder, liquorice strings and toffee chew bars sometimes. For a few years I would get gob-stoppers that were so big they nearly choked you trying to suck off the sugary layers and crack through to the one below, before taking it out of your

Gobstoppers were also known as 'jawbreakers'.

mouth to examine what colour it had turned into. But they were banned after the real risk of choking became recognised. My only near disaster was when I swallowed a polo whole, went very red and agitated though my brother watching from the other platform could do little about it. I remember claiming that I got air through the hole as it went down. The other tubes of sweets that I liked included Refreshers of pastel colours, slightly fizzy and crunchy, wine-gums (the black ones were the best), and coloured chocolate Smarties, hardly changed for 50 years.

I suppose after the war years there was a certain laissez-faire attitude to treats and sweets and my parents must have known that they could not supervise me on the way home from school. I was taken to the dentist every six months and I always cleaned my teeth night and morning in a token attempt to be good. Needless to say my teeth and gums were never very healthy and, as my genetic tendencies and fatigue from being a working mother may have contributed to the problem, I lost most of my teeth before I was 60. On the positive side, I had a lot of fun choosing, savouring, sharing sweets, saving or spending my pocket money, and I usually got home on time.

As this advertisement in a 1951 Home Notes magazine states, most women in their forties might have lost half their teeth.

January	Eden resigned as Prime Minister due to ill health and was succeeded by Harold Macmillan
February	Earthquake in East Midlands
March	**Treaty of Rome established European Economic Community (European Market)**
April	First televised April Fools Day joke, BBC showed tree harvest of spaghetti
	First BBC broadcast of *The Sky at Night* with Patrick Moore (still continuing)
May	Britain tested its first hydrogen bomb on a Pacific island
June	First Premium Bond winners selected by computer ERNIE
	Medical Research Council report provided hard evidence of link between smoking and lung cancer
July	Macmillan speech: "most of our people have never had it so good", followed by national strike of provincial bus drivers, with some violence
	Welsh village Capel Celyn drowned to form a reservoir for Liverpool
August	*Andy Capp* cartoons appeared in the *Daily Mirror*
	Fusion reactor started to operate at Harwell
September	**Wolfenden Report recommended homosexualism be decriminalised**
October	Asian flu vaccine introduced
	Russia launched Sputnik, the first man-made satellite: the start of the *Space Age*
	Fire at nuclear reactor at Windscale contaminated surrounding area with radioactivity
	Jodrell Bank Observatory became operational
November	First living animal in space, dog Laika, launched in

	Sputnik 2, but died before or during descent
December	Wales given its first Minister of State at Westminster
	Foot-and-mouth cattle disease reported in Liverpool abattoir

*Laika, the first dog in space,
launched on Soviet Sputnik 2,
November 1957.*

*The Vulcan B2 bomber of the RAF, first flown
in 1952, was used from 1957 to carry a nuclear
bomb due to the threat feared from the USSR
during the 'Cold War'.*

A Maltese idyll

Katie Wilkins

In 1957, three years after food rationing had finally ended in the UK, my father was posted to Malta for three years. He wasn't in the Navy but was a 'civilian attached', dealing with housing. And so it was that the house I had lived in up to that time was sold, some of the family possessions went into store, other possessions were crated up and sent ahead and eventually, in April of that year, when I was six years old, we all set off.

My parents had tried to give me an idea of where we were going, and I developed images of a wonderful little island bathed in eternal sun, full of friendly foreigners but surrounded by Her Majesty's Navy and so safe from invasion. I wasn't enthusiastic about leaving my friends and the only home I'd known, but the thought of this little paradise did soften the blow.

I had never been in an aeroplane before, and air travel wasn't at all sophisticated then. Malta is a very easy hop for modern airliners but, 54 years ago, you had to do it in two stages and in a very bumpy and uncomfortable plane. We flew from London to Nice, bouncing over the Alps with me standing in the aisle of the little plane screaming my head off. The cabin wasn't pressurised in the way modern aircraft are, and my ears hurt dreadfully. We landed in Nice and my mother had a very large brandy before we got on another plane for a smoother second leg of the journey.

When we landed I was sure we must be in the wrong place and I wondered if I should tell the pilot. It was pouring with rain and I remember being buffeted by the wind as we walked down the steps of the plane to the tarmac. My island bathed in uninterrupted sunshine was, initially, a terrible disappointment.

But things did get better. We lived in Villa Trafalgar, in Ta'Xbiex, between Sliema and Valletta. Overnight we had gone from a very modest house in north London to a large Mediterranean villa, with a room for our maid, a vine-covered courtyard at the back with geckos running up the wall, the warm inky blue Mediterranean sea just in front of us and yes, the sun did shine. A lot. Grey, austerity, Britain seemed a million miles away.

I'm told I was miserable for the first few months we were there, but I have no memory of this. I just have the most wonderful memories of growing up on Malta, of swimming every day, of playing outside with friends and of being like little savages in a wonderfully friendly and safe environment.

Our villa was on what we called 'the high road', and 'the low road' ran just below it, with steps between. I used to get home from school at lunchtime (we worked tropical hours in the summer), get into my swimming costume, shoot across the high road, down the steps, across the low road and onto the rocks, and dive into the sea. I learnt to swim soon after we arrived and I loved the water. I was given the nickname 'the little fish' because of the amount of time I spent in the water. I just used to swim out on my own, no-one worrying about the restrictions which would apply nowadays, and I absolutely loved it.

Ta'Xbiex was a main naval housing area so I was surrounded by other naval children with whom I quickly made friends. The high road gradually sloped down to join the low road in both directions, and we used to have roller skating races down the slopes, seeing who could get up the most speed by the time you got to the bottom. There was hardly any traffic and we didn't have any accidents other than a few scuffed knees.

There was also an open area close to the houses which we called the waste ground, and it was a favourite meeting place where we played and made up various 'clubs' we could belong to, with initiation ceremonies, vows of allegiance, and tasks we had to undertake to prove ourselves.

There was a year when money was being raised for a local worthy cause, and I got the idea of putting on 'The Wizard of Oz' to raise money. We had a large enough sitting-room to screen off one end with sheets as an acting area, and the local parents made up our audience. We wrote our own version of the story, which probably took all of ten minutes to perform, and I remember the fun and excitement of putting the script together. My best friend played the Wicked Witch of the West, my elder brother played the Wizard and I was the Tin Woodman. The Wicked Witch melts when water is thrown at her and my friend couldn't stop bursting into helpless laughter every time this happened in rehearsal. So we practised in our bathroom – her standing in the bath while I threw buckets of water over her. This, together with my first entrance as the Tin Woodman, when I was late because my mother was still pinning me into the many packs of baking foil I was dressed in, are lasting memories of my first theatrical adventure.

My father was a very talented sportsman, particularly in cricket; he played for Scotland as a young man. My parents joined the Marsa Club which was popular with everyone posted to Malta, and he played cricket there as often as he could. So we frequently went there as a family, and I used to go off climbing trees and swimming while Dad was playing.

I remember one afternoon with my best friend, when we met up with two of the boys we knew from school and broke into the squash courts at the club. We had no malicious intent, and we were careful not to damage anything, but I do remember the boys showing off to us by each demonstrating how far they could pee up the wall of one of the squash courts. I did feel rather guilty for the next people using that court, and I do hope the boys improved on their chat up techniques as they grew older.

Time came when my father's posting came to an end. There was no option of going back to the UK during Dad's tour of duty, so we children had spent three years isolated from what was going on back at home. I was frightened and very sad, knowing I had to leave this place where I had been so happy, as well as leaving all the friends I had made.

But it was interesting once we were back and, although it was undoubtedly colder and less sunny, I was struck by how green England is. I had lived for three years in a sandstone and blue coloured world, and the trees and flowers, the wonderful crunch of leaves under your feet in autumn, the variety of smells and light and shade, were so different.

And when I started school again people were talking about an American man called Elvis Presley. Everyone was talking about him. He was apparently very popular, he was a singer and girls swooned over him. But I had never heard of him. The world has become a very small place now, but it wasn't like that then.

1958

	Cod War between Britain and Iceland over a 12 mile fishing limit
	Carnaby Street, first clothes boutique for men
	Decline in baby boom began
	Bri-Nylon named
	BBC Radiophonic Workshop created
January	US launched space satellite Explorer 1
February	**Munich aircrash killed 21 people including several members of the Manchester United football team flying back from the European Cup in Belgrade**
	Loss of 2500 jobs with closure of Sheerness docks announced
	Campaign for Nuclear Disarmament (CND) launched; later USSR, USA and UK agree on three-year truce on atomic bomb tests
	Egypt and Syria formed the United Arab Republic
	Victorian Society held its first meeting for the preservation of Victorian architecture
	The first woman flight attendant appointed in US, but she lost her job when she married
March	**Vivian Fuchs completed first crossing of Antarctic in 99 days**
	First Planetarium in Britain opened, London
April	Three-day protest march to Aldermarston by CND
	Expo 58: World Fair in Brussels
June	*Lancet* **described diagnostic use of ultrasound**
July	Last formal presentation of debutantes to the Queen
	First parking meters introduced
	Prince Charles given title of Prince of Wales

	Iraqi monarchy overthrown
	Chinese-Tibet uprising
August	First Life Peer, Ian Fraser
	First woman peer, Barbara Wootton
	Notting Hill racial riots
	Nabokov's controversial book *Lolita* published
September	Severe storm in SE England disrupted communications
	Hire purchase restrictions relaxed
October	First jet passenger service across Atlantic, BOAC Comets
	First broadcast of sports programme *Grandstand*
	First broadcast of children's programme *Blue Peter*
	First TV broadcast of State Opening of Parliament
November	**Donald Campbell set water speed record, 248.62mph**
	World first: computer exhibition at Earls Court
December	Castro invaded Cuba
	The Queen inaugurated Subscriber Trunk Dialling (STD) with a call from Bristol to Edinbugh
	Britain's first motorway opened, Preston by-pass

Donald Campbell in his water-speed record-braking craft 'Bluebird'.

Police with traffic sleeves

Donald Davis

Do you ever think about the days when policemen were policemen, not speeding about the town with electronic sirens blaring fit to wake the dead? Once a policeman was a nice man who nodded to you as you went past, standing in the middle of a busy junction directing the traffic in a calm, almost casual way but with the skill of an expert. Resplendent in his uniform with its white 'traffic' sleeves, his pointed helmet and the discreet leather strap of his truncheon peeping out of the hidden pocket in his trousers, to me he epitomised all that was right in a world seemingly safe and unstressed.

Now we have policemen patrolling in twos in my quiet seaside town of Worthing, weighed down with items of both defence and offence. Bare armed, their hands are thrust aggressively into the arm-holes of their anti-stab jackets. With black combat trousers tucked military-style into their boots, their belts are visibly adorned by pepper spray, handcuffs, taser gun and truncheon. "If you want to know the time ask a policemen" they say, but his colleague, talking into his collar, will first warn his controller that they have been approached by a member of the public who wants to know the time! 'Suspect behaviour, Sarg ?'

Perhaps Grumpy Old Men like me need to get 'with it' as they say. 'Get a life Dad!' Language has changed over the years, not even years perhaps but days: 'Now that's cool'. *Cool'* can mean just about anything you want it to mean. Cool, man!

Consider the number of people who no longer live in, or even near, the place where they were born. I know populations are more mobile now than they used to be, but there has to be a reason why so many, particularly men, moved hundreds of miles from the family home, married there and raised a family. National Service was responsible. It was the biggest population shift since the Romans chased the English into Wales. Able-bodied, fit young men found themselves stationed in areas they would normally never have visited and, out of the clutches of their parents, foot-loose and fancy-free, earnestly sought out the attentions of the opposite sex.

In the early 1960s 'ready to play' plastic toys were coming onto the market. They didn't need much skill to operate compared with the playthings we had as children. Remember the Whip and Top? We had league tables at school as to who could keep one going the longest or furthest (from home to school without stopping).

There were also Conkers and Marbles, pastimes that formed friendships for life or perhaps the very opposite if you were too good. Marbles was played either in a circle on a bit of sandy ground, where you attempted to knock your opponents' marbles out of the ring, or in a straight line along the gutter on the way to school. This method had problems. Two in fact. You often ended with scratched and bleeding knees through over zealous contact with the pavement. Or, much worse, you were terribly late for school. That was bad news. Assembly had already started but on the arrival of the headmaster you were unceremoniously given three (at least) strokes of the cane on each palm. That hurt, but it didn't stop us playing marbles.

Much of what I have touched upon here would be banned under legislation that seems to leap out of the European Parliament at the drop of a hat. I'm sure the 'combat' dress of our policemen has little to do with the safety of police officers, but more about their superiors protecting themselves from the threat of litigation. Likewise Conkers is now banned but not for the protection of the poor old chestnut tree but the protection of

Council Health and Safety executives. Caning (smacking) children? Well there's now a hundred laws to prevent that, starting with their human rights and ending with those departments dealing with what is sinisterly termed 'Child Abuse'.

Writing this article on a laptop computer has given me much room for thought. In a split second I can be connected to someone on the other side of the world. Whatever I question, whatever I seek, the answer is instantly at my finger tips. What an amazing invention: what a profound experience! I doubt there has ever been anything in all of history that has had such a mind-boggling impact on the human race, apart from perhaps the discovery of fire.

I recall my mother telling me that when she was a little girl someone had invented a thing called a wireless. You could hear people talking and music playing, the sound just came through the air she said, all by itself and into something called a receiver in your home. 'It was almost like magic', she said. With the advent of the computer I now know how amazed she was. So from this little acorn the mighty oak of the Computer was born, now routinely taken for granted by the young, as the radio was by me.

There have been so many changes, some mind bending and frightening like the atomic bomb. Aircraft can now fly at 2000 miles per hour. Space ships can put a man on the moon and may shortly put men on other moons. Just where will it all end? I would dearly love to hear the comments of people who might be reading this in, say, 200 years time.

I suppose Columbus looking at America through his telescope might have wondered just how stupid were those who thought the world was flat.

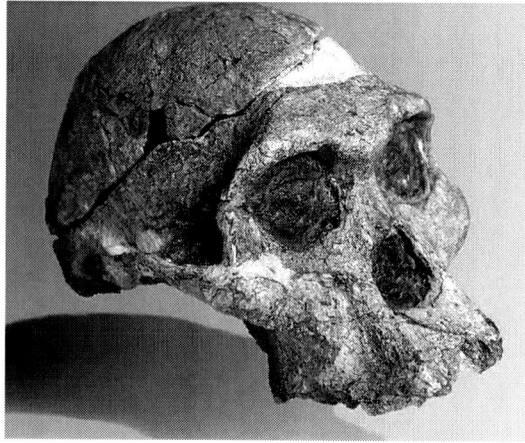

An australopithecus skull. In 1959 Mary Leakey was the first to discover a specimen of this hominid ancestor of homo sapiens in Tanzania.

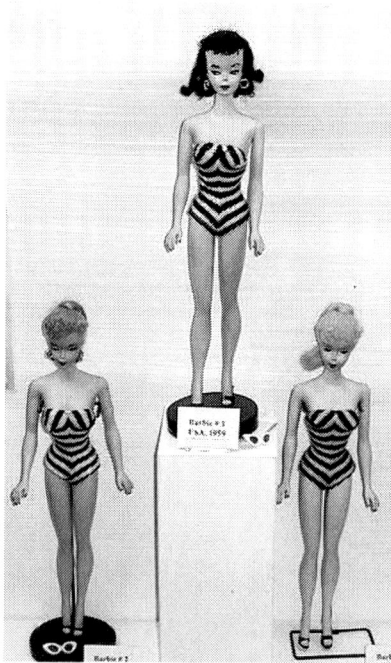

In 1959 (in stark contrast) the Barbie Doll was first offered for sale.

1959

	First recorded human death from HIV, Congo
	Alaska and Hawaii joined the USA as the 49th and 50th states
	Pantyhose first went on sale
January	Dense fog brings chaos in Britain
	Prime Minister Macmillan met Soviet leader Khrushchev in Russia
February	Switzerland referendum rejected votes for women
	First successful test of an intercontinental ballistic missile, Cape Canaveral
	Castro became Premier of Cuba
March	Barbie doll went on sale
April	Icelandic gunboat fired on British trawlers
May	CP Snow delivered lecture on *The Two Cultures* identifying a breakdown between science and humanities
	Two monkeys were the first live primates to return safely from space, Jupiter AM18
	Import tariffs lifted in UK
June	First hovercraft launched
July	**Post codes introduced**
	The Leakeys discovered the first Australopithecus skull in Tanzania
	Venus occulted the star Regulus, revealing Venus' diameter and atmosphere
August	**Explorer 6 sends the first pictures of earth from space**
	The first Mini car went on sale
October	**Soviet Luna 3 photographed the far side of the moon**

	300 people rescued from a fire on Southend Pier
	Margaret Thatcher became an MP in the General Election
	Large scale diamond robbery in London
November	First part of the M1 motorway opened between Watford and Rugby
	Britain became a founder member of the European Free Trade Association
December	Health advocate Dr Barbara Moore walked from Edinburgh to London
	Charles de Gaulle elected president of France
	Antarctica declared a scientific reserve

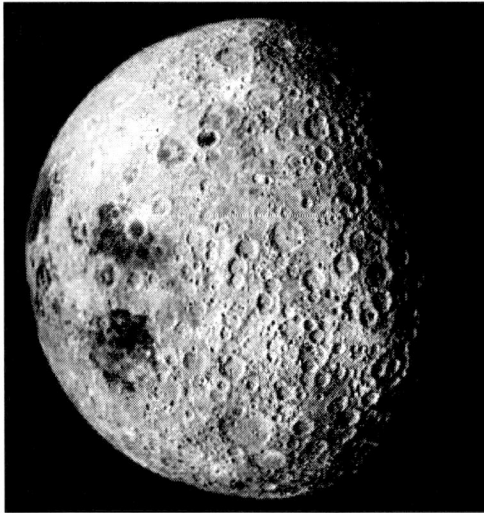

The far side of the moon, first photographed in 1959.

Instructing the police

Mark Johnson

On April 1st 1947 my service in the Royal Navy ended. I had spent one year in Britain and two years overseas from the age of 17 to 20. Demobbed North East naval personnel were sent to Fulford Road Army Barracks in York. There, under the guidance of a Regimental Sergeant Major, we were issued with civilian clothing, demob suits and a few other essentials. Unfortunately I had outgrown all my civilian clothes, and had to be helped by using my parents' clothing coupons.

My father had served 32 years as a constable in Newcastle City Police (including four years of army service in the First World War). So I followed in his footsteps and joined the Newcastle City Police, exchanging one blue uniform for a different blue. For my first eight years I was a constable on the beat, and then had two years out of uniform on the Vice Squad in City West. After promotion to sergeant in City Central, I spent six years first on uniformed patrol, then the Vice Squad again and finally Station Sergeant. Here I accepted charges daily which ranged from the mundane, such as shoplifting and being drunk and disorderly, to the serious such as murder and rape.

After six months at the Police College in Hampshire I was promoted to Inspector, and returned to where I had started, Newcastle City West. Then came the call for a two-year secondment for training as an Inspector Instructor in Harrogate, at a former public school which had a large sports field, rugby pitches and an indoor swimming pool. For two years I made about

100 journeys travelling the 84 miles between Harrogate and Newcastle, home on Friday evening and returning on Sunday evening. The disadvantage was that my wife had to care for our three children, aged 11, 7 and 1, on her own, but the advantage was a salary a rank above one's grade, a very fair petrol allowance, and a further promotion in due course.

The organisation at Harrogate catered for 240 constables – all male. The Syndicates (a posh word for classes) consisted of 20 constables, a Commandant (Chief Superintendent), his Deputy (Superintendent), four Inspectors each with three Sergeants and twenty Probationer Constables. The courses were in three stages: four weeks at Junior level, eight at Intermediate and twelve at Senior.

I recall giving a lecture on Section 1 of the Sexual Offences Act (Rape) when I sensed someone was at the classroom door. I strode over to it and opened it with the result that the two female cleaners who had been eavesdropping fell into the room. They ran off along the corridor. Other female staff got into more serious trouble. At two in the morning there was a report of intruders in the female domestics' building. The fire escape door had been deliberately left open. Two constables were carpeted and reprimanded. Two junior female kitchen staff were dismissed; they had been a source of trouble previously.

On a more serious note, a young constable returning from Lincoln on his motor cycle on a wet Sunday evening broke down in Wetherby. A kindly motorist offered him a lift to the Training Centre. As they drove into Harrogate a pedestrian stepped off the footpath in front of the car and was killed instantly. I was Duty Officer that night.

A monthly fire drill was held at the Centre on different dates and times. On one occasion it seemed to have gone off perfectly, with everyone present and correct on the parade ground. But perfect it turned out not to be. A constable was in Sick Bay with a broken leg from playing football, and the Training Centre's nurse had gone into town without informing anybody. At another time we had a visit from a Detective Inspector from the local constabulary. It seemed that one of our probationer constables of previously blameless character had been breaking into premises with another man on his weekend leave. The probationer requested his Syndicate Sergeant to sit in for the interview, and he made a correct, written, voluntary statement admitting all the offences. He was arrested, charged and convicted. His police career lasted only a few weeks.

Finally, for the rest of us, came the Passing Out Parade. This was always a spectacular occasion with the Leeds City Police Band, and included a physical education display and a drill parade, watched by mums, dads, wives and sweethearts. It was followed by a buffet paid for by the Police Student Welfare Fund. Then everyone was gone to all points in Yorkshire, Derbyshire, Lincolnshire, Nottinghamshire and the North East. After a touch of nostalgia, everything was then got ready for a fresh intake of sixty Probationer Constables on the following Monday.

On returning from Harrogate I rejoined my Force, Newcastle City Police. When traffic wardens were introduced to Newcastle I had a spell in charge of seventy of them.

Two years later the Newcastle Police Force amalgamated with Northumbria, and it was with them that I finished my police career after 31 years of service (nearly as long as my father's) and with the rank of Chief Inspector.

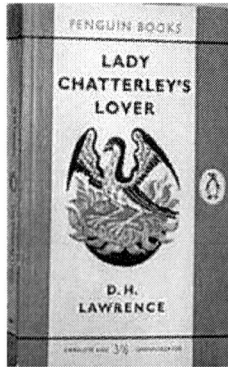

In 1960 Penguin publishers won a famous trial when 'Lady Chatterley's Lover' was found not to be obscene.

The Beatles made their first major appearance in 1960 in Hamburg. This photo is of them landing in New York in 1964.

1960

	Several African states gained independence, including Somaliland, Nigeria, Niger, Congo, Zambia, Ivory Coast, Ghana, Madagascar, Mauritania, Chad
	MOTs instituted, cars over 10 years old to have brakes, lights and steering tested every year
January	Kenya state of emergency lifted and Mau-Mau rising was officially over
February	Macmillan made *Wind of Change* speech in Cape Town
	CERN particle accelerator began operating in Geneva
	The Queen's third child born
March	**Sharpeville massacre in S Africa**
	3,500 American troops sent to Vietnam
	The laser was patented
	Swiss Canton Geneva allowed women to vote
April	Mass production of British Blue Streak missile was cancelled
	US launched the first weather satellite
	Elvis Presley cut his first record, *Are You Lonely Tonight?*
May	**The first contraceptive pill *Enovid* was approved in US**
	Massive earthquake and tsunami in Chile
July	Francis Chichester completed record solo Atlantic crossing by sail in 40 days
	For the first time Woolworth's served a black customer a meal
August	Bluebell Railway became the world's first steam-operated heritage railway

	The Beatles performed in Hamburg
September	**First traffic wardens, London**
	Severe floods in Devon
	First televised debate between Presidential candidates, Nixon and Kennedy
October	Severe floods in Lincolnshire
	Britain's first nuclear submarine launched, *HMS Dreadnoiught*
	First successful kidney transplant in Britain, Edinburgh
	Cassius Clay (later to be Muhammed Ali) won his first professional boxing match
November	*Lady Chatterley's Lover* declared not obscene, sold 200,000 copies in one day
December	*Coronation Street's* first showing on ITV
	Farthings no longer legal tender, first minted in the 13th century
	Record flight-altitude 27,674m in a twin-jet bomber
	Last man called up for National Service, as conscription ended

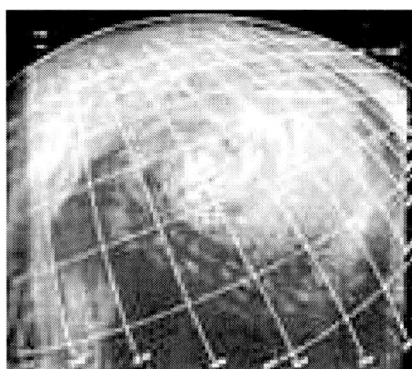

A cyclone on earth; picture sent from the first weather satellite, TIROS-1, in 1960.

Codicil: End of Empire

Elspeth Jones

At the age of ten, my life was changed utterly and for ever. Until 1962, when my father decided to uproot our family and move to East Africa, we had lived an ordinary life in suburban Lancashire – father in the Civil Service, mother a part-time teacher, older brother at the Grammar School across town. I was still at the local primary school.

But then came the bombshell. Dad was to go first, Mum and I to follow – all by sea (hardly anyone flew then) and brother Richard was to go to the boarding wing at his school, to prepare for his 'A' levels.

So, there we were. Mum started packing and making lists. Granny P (Dad's mother) got ready to move into our house with a housekeeper. I looked up East Africa in the set of Children's Encyclopaedias in the book-case, and my father eventually left. It seemed all of a piece with his character that he didn't go the usual way from Southampton on one of the 'Castle ' liners that still plied their way round colonial Africa. Oh, no! He wanted to take the train across Europe to join a smaller Italian vessel at Genoa, which, after much discussion with the Crown Office, he did. It still took him three weeks to reach Dar es Salaam, in Tanganyika as it was known then (now Tanzania), where he settled into a bachelor life, working by day as a telephone manager and sailing at the Dar Club in the evenings.

Mum and I set sail from Southampton at the end of November. I don't remember how my brother Richard felt, pretty shattered I imagine, but Granny was in the wings and I found out, in middle age, after our parents died, that they offered each other companionship and that Richard soon left the school to live back at home with her. It was to be a part of my experience from that time that I had to piece together bits about our family in this way: hurriedly; at funerals; asking awkward questions; finding the family cache of letters from Africa during the war; writing poetry and memoirs. All this was to make sense of a childhood that had lost all security, all the things children usually expect.

At the time, however, I was an excited ten-year-old with a new life beginning. Right up until our departure, I had been a very fussy eater. But, as we sat down to dinner, during that never-to-be forgotten thirty-day voyage, I began to see the error of my ways. The tables were large, round and beautifully set with white cloths and serviettes and gleaming silver. I would look at the elaborate menu, and at the others round the table all in, what seemed to me, Sunday best every single night. Taking a deep breath, I ordered outlandish things like 'beef bourguignon' and 'consommé', whilst whispering to Mum for help when the spotlight was off me.

Once the Bay of Biscay was passed and Gibraltar reached, the weather warmed up and we gradually forgot the cold and dark of a British December. Sailing through the Med was a revelation to a little girl, whose holidays had previously been in Cornwall or Wales. I would spend hours stationary at the rail, watching the foamy swell pass under the ship. Once Stromboli was past (that little volcanic island just south of Sicily), we seemed to be entering another world. On reaching Egypt, we berthed at Port Said and, whilst the Braemar Castle sailed through the Suez Canal, took 'A Quick Trip to Cairo' as my mother always called it. We had reached Dad's hallowed Africa at last.

Cairo was hotter than I had ever thought possible. We stayed at the Mena House Hotel, which had long dim corridors and quiet servants in white robes and red fezzes. Our set of rooms was larger than our whole house at home. But where was home? I was no longer sure.

However, I was beginning to enjoy this new thing called 'travel' and wanted to go on, not back. We saw the Sphinx and the Pyramids at Giza, (with Mum very brave riding on a camel) and Tutankhamun in the Cairo Museum – all old hat now, but I had only seen them in my set of encyclopaedias.

On, on went the Braemar Castle, down the Red Sea, calling at Aden and, at last, Mombasa in Kenya. Dad was there to meet us. I could see him from the deck and, in a classic thirties Hollywood moment, waved before walking calmly down to meet him, and saying politely: 'Hello, Daddy'. Rubbish! I was so excited I felt sick and pelted down all the decks and into his arms.

During our journey, our destination had miraculously changed. We were no longer to sail on to Dar es Salaam, but travel 300 miles inland to Nairobi, the capital of Kenya (always pronounced 'Keenya' then), and 6000 feet up in the air. In the early 1960s, Kenya, Tanganyika and Uganda still made up the colony of East Africa, and Dad had found it fairly easy to transfer to Nairobi. But why? With the uncurious stare of childhood I didn't ask, but found out later that there had been a real concern about Mum's health if she stayed at the coast. Hence the change. In fact she thrived, as the photos show. Always a beauty (a word still used in those days), her olive skin became deeply tanned and she enjoyed the life of a ' company wife', providing a home for Dad and me, playing golf and tennis, swimming, writing home to Richard, Granny and her own father - even teaching part time and, of course, preparing for Richard's holiday visits.

We lived in a government-allotted house, about 15 minutes from the centre of town. The houses were pleasant, anonymous bungalows, but what a setting! On the side of a slope, the garden was full of bougainvillea, and the mauve flowered jacaranda trees. From the veranda we looked over a wooded valley with a stream flowing down from the Highlands. I could see the red roof of my school from the top of the tree that I used to climb. The children on our road were called the 'valley children' and, for most of the year, walked across the stream to school with ease. However, when the rainy season threatened, we came home early, as the stream soon became a torrent and Dad had to take me five miles round. This was a bit different from Lancashire, I think now, but was all accepted then.

What else do I remember? – brother Richard flying out for the school holidays, telling me about the Beatles and playing 'I Like It' very loud on a dancette in the garden; our servant, Jonas, taking us to the Kikuyu heartland, proudly introducing us to his three wives and 16 children and showing Dad and Richard his four acres of coffee; careering all over Kenya and Tanganyika in Dad's car on atrocious roads, sometimes having to push it out of mud or through streams; needing to carry a glue called 'gun gum' for repairs to the sump; driving to Mombasa with a home-made boat on the roof, that fell off and was never seen again; standing with Richard at the Equator sign on the road north to Eldoret; my first taste of pau-pau, a bit like Gallia melon but sweeter and more luscious; Jonas whacking grass snakes in the garden; huge spiders hiding in the loo; experiencing the sudden equatorial darkness at 6pm; playing 'dummy' whist in the evenings after Richard had gone home to England; playing teenage dolls with a friend, both of us on the cusp of girlhood; Richard, again, climbing Kilimanjaro at age 16, long before Comic Relief was ever thought of; the four of us facing up to a mad buffalo in the Serengeti; watching the fireworks for Uhuru (independence), which spelled the end of our time there; and, finally, the telephone call that summoned Mum back to England for her own daddy's funeral. This was our very own End of Empire, as she found the lady who looked after Granny took the opportunity to give notice.

This meant we had to come home six months earlier than the usual two-year 'tour'. It seemed indicative of the 'wind of change' sweeping over Africa that we flew back, rather than by another iconic sea voyage. There was some talk of transferring to Botswana, but I think Mum put her foot down and so we returned

214

to a green land with small houses and a familiar chill, even in summer.

Truly, life was never to be the same again. For one thing, my accent had turned from broad Lancs to posh. I said 'baath' not 'bath', and 'paas' not 'pass. Tanned, fit and leggy, my hair bleached blonde from the African sun, I had my old friend on the street stunned. He would just stand by the gate and look. My childhood was nearly over. I never seemed to fit in to that quiet Lancashire town after our adventures. Perhaps this was fortuitous as, hardly able to draw breath, our travels continued. Richard went to university and Dad had one more move in northern England, waiting for a promotion. Then we moved on to Northern Ireland two years before 'The Troubles' began. I was thirteen years old. Another chapter had begun.

It would take another thirteen years of travelling to find that home is where you make it; not a place, but an attitude of mind; that travelling hones the ability to push into the unknown; that, with time, there comes the chutzpah to be resilient and choose friends wisely. After much searching, and with a certain wisdom, I realised I could find my own safe harbour to replace the one lost whilst gazing over the rail on a long voyage to the End of Empire.

Survival

Trish Kent

First, we survived being born to mothers who smoked and/or drank while they carried us and lived in houses made of asbestos. They took aspirin, ate blue cheese, raw egg products, loads of bacon and processed meat, tuna from a can and didn't get tested for diabetes or cervical cancer. Then after that trauma, our baby cots were covered with bright coloured lead-based paint.

We had no child-proof lids on medicine bottles, doors or cabinets and when we rode our bikes we had no helmets, not to mention the risks we took hitchhiking. As children we would ride in cars with no seatbelts or airbags.

We drank water from the garden hose and not from a bottle. We shared soft drinks with four friends from one bottle and no-one actually died from this.

Take-away food was limited to fish and chips, no pizza shops, McDonalds, KFCs, Subways or Nandos. Even though all the shops closed at 6pm, had half-day closing on Wednesdays and didn't open on the weekends, somehow we didn't starve to death. We ate cupcakes, white bread and real butter and drank soft drinks with sugar in them, but we weren't overweight because we were always outside playing.

Grocers in the mid-century sometimes kept their flour in large tin bins such as this, weighing out the amount the customer needed and packing it into a brown paper bag. This particular bin was used by a Yorkshire mill weaver to supply flour to her neighbours in the village.

We could collect old drinks bottles and cash them in at the corner store and buy toffees, gobstoppers, bubble gum and some bangers to blow up frogs with.

We would leave home in the morning and play all day, as long as we were home when the street-lights came on. No one was able to reach us all day. And we were OK. We would spend hours building our go-karts out of old prams and then ride downhill, only to find out we forgot the brakes. We built tree houses and dens and played in river beds with matchbox cars.

We didn't have Playstations, Nintendo Wii, X-boxes; we had no video games at all, no 999 channels on Sky, no video/DVD films, no mobile phones, no personal computers, no Internet or Internet chat rooms. We had friends and we went outside and found them! We fell out of trees, got cut, broke bones and teeth and there were no lawsuits from these accidents. We ate worms and mud pies made from dirt and the worms did not live in us forever.

You could only buy Easter Eggs and Hot Cross Buns at Easter time.

Only girls had pierced ears.

We were given airguns and catapults for our 10th birthdays. We rode bikes or walked to a friend's house and knocked on the door or rang the bell or just yelled for them.

Mum didn't have to go to work to help Dad make ends meet.

Rugby and cricket had tryouts and not everyone made the team. Those who didn't had to learn to deal with disappointment. Imagine that! Getting into a team was based on merit.

Our teachers used to hit us with canes and gymshoes, and bullies *always* ruled the playground at school. The idea of a parent bailing us out if we broke the law was unheard of. They actually sided with the law.

Our parents didn't invent stupid names for their kids like *Kiora* and *Blade* and *Ridge* and *Vanilla*.

We had freedom, failure, success and responsibility and learned how to deal with it all.

Acknowledgements and thanks for the illustrations to

Huntley Hedworth
Corinne Lesser
The authors
Wikipedia

and admiration and gratitude also to the contributors to this book who have shared their memories and delved into their albums and treasure boxes. Warm thanks especially to Jim Edwardson and to the members of Newcastle U3A's Publications Team, particularly the proof-readers.

The authors

Most of the authors of this book are members of Newcastle U3A (University of the Third Age).

U3As are amazingly economical ways of helping people to keep mentally, physically and socially active. They do this by consisting entirely of volunteers who share their knowledge, skills and experience and learn from each other. They are the fun side of learning without the essays or exams. Anyone retired can join. No qualifications are required and none are given. They are not-for-profit charities.

The hundreds of autonomous U3As together form the only national educational organisation in Britain run entirely by its own (250,000+) members.

The many U3As throughout the world have a growing membership pursuing a very broad range of topics – in Newcastle, for example, from Computing and Latin to Ukuleles and Watercolours. The production of this book is another example.

Newcastle U3A, Unit 3, 1 Pink Lane, Newcastle upon Tyne, NE1 5DW, UK Tel:(44)(0) 191 230 4430   newcastleu3a@hotmail.com www.nru3a.co.uk   Registered UK Charity No 1078961